# NATURE'S RAGE
## IN THE
# CARIBBEAN

Norma Iris Pagan Morales

ISBN 978-1-959895-33-6 (paperback)
ISBN 978-1-959895-32-9 (ebook)

Printed in the United States of America

WEST POINT
PRINT AND MEDIA

# ACKNOWLEDGEMENT

Dedicated to my dear sister, Adelin Milagros Pagan Morales. She worried so much during Hurricane Maria. Hurricane Maria hit Puerto Rico on September 20, 2017. Five years later, Fiona…

# OVERVIEW

There is no place for politics during an emergency. Politics play a role in how the Caribbean is managing during the tumultuous hurricane season.

The longtime colonial rule isn't the only reason Caribbean societies and ecosystems are now so defenseless. Many modern governments in the region are doing their part in making life generally worse for the downgraded communities.

From Jamaica to Belize, there is a widespread of corruption. There are rights violations. There is also a severe relationship of trust between people and the states. In theory, the government is assigned to protect its people when there are storms threaten.

The policies and practices intensify the Caribbean's shared and environmental risks. To survive and flourish in this dangerous new normal, Caribbean countries would do well if they look at these issues. They must rethink at the concept of risk and mindfully engage with factors like poverty, gender, and climate change.

Puerto Rico is not exempt from the above-mentioned politics or any other source of the so-called protection.

# CONTENTS

# CHAPTER 1

# Tsunami, Hurricane, Cyclone, Typhoo, and Tropical storms

In this chapter, there is inside material that must be share! This unique information will save lives and I mean hundreds of lives.

I began the chapter with questions and answers. It does not matter if you live in the Caribbean or in the states.

If you are a teacher, you may use it in your classroom, however, as a parent, this information is vital....

## What is a Tsunami?

A tsunami is a series of waves caused by earthquakes or undersea volcanic eruptions.

Tsunamis are giant waves caused by earthquakes or volcanic eruptions under the sea. Out in the depths of the ocean, tsunami waves do not dramatically increase in height. But as the waves travel inland, they build up to higher and higher heights as the depth of the ocean decreases.

The speed of tsunami waves depends on ocean depth rather than the distance from the source of the wave. Tsunami waves may travel as fast as jet planes over deep waters, only slowing down when reaching shallow waters. While tsunamis are often referred to as tidal waves, this name is discouraged by oceanographers because tides have little to do with these giant waves.

## Can Puerto Rico have a tsunami?

The danger of <u>a tsunami in Puerto Rico is real</u>. Since 1867, two tsunamis have affected their coastal region, causing death and destruction in 1867 and 1918.

Although the source of these tsunamis has been earthquakes, a tsunami can also be generated by an underwater landslide, a volcanic eruption, and the impact from a meteorite. However, in the case of Puerto Rico, an eruption is little likely to occur.

## What is a hurricane?

A hurricane is an enormous storm! It can be up to 600 miles across and have strong winds spiraling inward and upward at speeds of 75 to 200 mph. Each hurricane usually lasts for over a week, moving 10-20 miles per hour over the open ocean.

Hurricanes gather heat and energy through contact with warm ocean waters. Evaporation from the seawater increases their power. Hurricanes rotate in a counterclockwise direction around an "eye" in the Northern Hemisphere and clockwise direction in the Southern Hemisphere.

The center of the storm or "eye" is the calmest part. It has only light winds and fair weather. When they come on land, the heavy rain, strong winds and large waves can damage buildings, trees, and cars.

## How do hurricanes form?

Hurricanes only form over warm ocean water of 80°F or warmer. The atmosphere, the air, must cool off very quickly the higher you go. Also, the wind must be blowing in the same direction and at the same speed to force air upward from the ocean surface.

Winds flow outward above the storm allowing the air below to rise. Hurricanes typically form between 5 to 15 degrees latitude north and south of the equator. The Coriolis force is needed to create the spin in the hurricane, and it becomes too weak near the equator, so hurricanes can never form there.

## What is storm surge?

Storm surges are frequently the most devastating element of a hurricane. As a hurricane's winds spiral around and around the storm, they push water into a mound at the storm's center.

This mound of water becomes dangerous when the storm reaches land because it causes flooding along the coast. The water piles up, unable to escape anywhere but on land as the storm carries it landward. A hurricane will cause more storm surge in areas where the ocean floor slopes gradually. This causes major flooding.

If you look at a storm-surge animation, you will notice the effect that the physical geography of each coastline has on storm surge. Also, note the waves on top of the ocean's surface. Wind, waves, and sea-level rise all contribute to storm-surge damage.

With technology the way it is, there are computer models that allow forecasters to predict the amount of storm surge that will affect a coastal area. These are called Slosh Models and consider a storm's strength, its path, how the ocean shallows, and the shape of the land. Then it calculates how much storm surge a hurricane will probably cause.

## When does hurricane season start?

The Atlantic hurricane season is from June 1 to November 30, but most hurricanes occur during the fall months. The Eastern Pacific hurricane season is from May 15 to November 30.

## Who names hurricanes?

From 1950 to 1952, tropical cyclones of the North Atlantic Ocean were identified by the phonetic alphabet, Able-Baker-Charlie-etc., but in 1953 the US Weather Bureau switched to women's names.

The rest of the world eventually caught on, and naming rights now go by the World Meteorological Organization, which uses different sets of names depending on the part of the world the storm is in.

Around the U.S., only women's names were used until 1979, when it was decided that they should alternate a list that included men's names too. There are 6 different name lists that alternate each year.

If a hurricane does considerable damage, its name is retired and replaced with another.

## What is the difference between a hurricane and a typhoon?

Nothing except geography. Tropical storms occur in several of the world's oceans, and except for their names, they are essentially the same type of storm.

In the Atlantic Ocean, Gulf of Mexico, and the Eastern Pacific Ocean, they are called hurricanes. In the Western Pacific Ocean, they are called typhoons. In the Indian Ocean, the Bay of Bengal, and Australia, these types of storms are called cyclones.

## Who are the "Hurricane Hunters"?

The brave "hurricane hunters" work for the National Oceanic and Atmospheric Administration, NOAA.

Each mission lasts about ten hours, with the crews passing four to six times through the storm. The planes carry radar, sophisticated computers, and weather instruments that determine characteristics such as temperature, air pressure, wind speed, and wind direction inside the hurricane.

The crews also release instruments that measure temperature, air pressure, and wind at different levels as the devices drop through the hurricane toward the ocean. By mission's end, NOAA can warn everyone about the hurricanes.

## What is coastal beach erosion?

Coastal beach erosion is the wearing a way of land, the removal of beach or dune sediments by wave action, tidal currents, wave currents, or drainage. Waves are generated by storms, wind, or hurricanes and can cause coastal erosion. This may take the form of long-term losses of sediment and rocks, or merely the temporary redistribution of coastal sediments.

# Hurricane Safety Tips

## Everyone must do this before and during hurricane season

You must have a disaster plan and a pet plan. Before a storm threatens, contact your veterinarian or local humane society for information on preparing your pets for an emergency. Board up windows and bring in outdoor objects that could blow away. Make sure you know which county or parish you live in and know where all the evacuation routes are.

Prepare a disaster supplies kit for your home and car. Include a first aid kit, canned food, and a can opener, bottled water, battery-operated radio, flashlight, protective clothing, and written instructions on how to turn off electricity, gas, and water.

You must have a NOAA weather radio handy with plenty of batteries, so you can listen to storm advisories.

It is a must to have some cash handy as well, because following a hurricane, banks and ATMs may be temporarily closed. Make sure your car is filled with gasoline.

## During a hurricane

Stay away from low-lying and flood prone areas. Always stay indoors during a hurricane because fierce winds will blow things around. Leave mobile homes and to go to a shelter. If your home is not on higher ground, go to a shelter. If emergency managers say to evacuate, then do so immediately.

## After a hurricane

Stay indoors until it is safe to come out. Check for injured or trapped people, without putting yourself in danger. Watch out for flooding which can happen after a hurricane. Do not attempt to drive in flooding water. Stay away from standing water. It may be electrically charged from underground or downed power lines. Don't drink tap water until officials say it's safe to do so.

## Hurricane vs. Typhoon

A hurricane is any mass of air that spirals around a low-pressure center. It is an organized collection of thunderstorms embedded in a swirling mass of air.

In general, both typhoons and hurricanes are tropical cyclones but differ in their locations. The difference between hurricane and typhoon is that tropical cyclones in the west Pacific are called Typhoons and those in the Atlantic and east Pacific Ocean are called Hurricanes. It's the longitude that matters.

## Hurricane

A hurricane is a cyclone that is in the North Atlantic Ocean, or the NE Pacific Ocean east of the International Date Line, or the South Pacific Ocean east of 160E, and with sustained winds that reach or exceed 74 mph.

Tropical cyclones in the Northwest Pacific Ocean west of the International Date Line with sustained winds of 74 mph are typhoons.

Even though I live in a tropical island, I am going to give you some useful information about tornados.

## What is a tornado?

A tornado is a violent rotating column of air extending from a thunderstorm to the ground. The most violent tornadoes are capable of tremendous destruction with wind speeds of up to three hundred mph. They can destroy large buildings, uproot trees, and hurl vehicles hundreds of yards. They can also drive straw into trees. Damage paths can be more than one mile wide to fifty miles long. In an average year, 1000tornadoes are reported nationwide.

## How do tornadoes form?

Most tornadoes form from thunderstorms. You need warm, moist air from the Gulf of Mexico and cool, dry air from Canada. When these two air masses meet, they create instability in the atmosphere. A change in wind direction and an increase in wind speed with increasing height creates an invisible, horizontal spinning effect in the lower atmosphere. Rising air within the updraft tilts the rotating air from horizontal to vertical. An area of rotation, 2-6 miles wide, now extends through much of the storm. Most strong and violent tornadoes form within this area of strong rotation.

## What do tornadoes look like?

Tornadoes can appear as a traditional funnel shape, or in a slender rope-like form. Some have a churning, smoky look to them, and other contain "multiple vortices", which are small, individual tornadoes rotating around a common center. Even others may be nearly invisible, with only swirling dust or debris at ground levels as the only indication of the tornado's presence.

## What is a funnel cloud?

A funnel cloud is a rotating cone-shaped column of air extending downward from the base of a thunderstorm, but not touching the ground. When it reaches the ground, it is called a tornado.

## How do tornadoes stop?

It is not fully understood about how exactly tornadoes form, grow and die. Tornado researchers are still trying to solve the tornado puzzle, but for every piece that seems to fit they often uncover new pieces that need to be studied.

## What is a super cell thunderstorm?

A super cell thunderstorm is a long-lived thunderstorm whose updrafts and downdrafts are in near balance. These storms have the greatest tendency to produce tornadoes that stay on the ground for long periods of time. Super cell thunderstorms can produce violent tornadoes with winds exceeding 200 mph.

## What is a mesocyclone?

A mesocyclone is a rotating vortex of air within a super cell thunderstorm. Mesocyclones do not always produce tornadoes.

## What is a microburst?

A microburst is a downdraft, sinking air, in a thunderstorm that is less than 2.5 miles in scale. Although microbursts are not as widely recognized as tornadoes, they can cause comparable, and in some cases, worse damage than some tornadoes produce. In fact, wind speeds as high as 150 mph are possible in extreme microburst cases.

## What is a wall cloud?

A wall cloud is an abrupt lowering of a rain-free cumulonimbus base into a low-hanging accessory cloud. A wall cloud is usually situated in the southwest portion of the storm. A rotating wall cloud usually develops before tornadoes or funnel clouds.

## What is a waterspout?

A waterspout is just a weak tornado that forms over water. They are most common along the Gulf Coast. Waterspouts can sometimes move inland, becoming tornadoes causing damage and injuries.

## What is the largest hailstone recorded in the United States?

According to the National Weather Service, the largest hailstone is 8 inches in diameter and weighs approximately 2 pounds. It fell in Vivian, South Dakota on July 23, 2010.

## What is hail?

Hail is created when small water droplets are caught in the updraft of a thunderstorm. These water droplets are lifted higher and higher into the sky until they freeze into ice. Once they become heavy, they will start to fall. If the smaller hailstones get caught in the updraft again, they will get more water on them and get lifted higher in the sky and get bigger. Once they get lifted again, they freeze and fall. This happens repeatedly until the hailstone is too heavy and then falls to the ground.

## What is a land spout?

A land spout is a very weak tornado that is not associated with a wall cloud or a mesocyclone. It is the land equivalent of a waterspout.

## What is a dust devil?

A dust devil generally forms in the hot sun during the late morning or early afternoon hours. These are mostly harmless whirlwinds and are triggered by light desert breezes that create a swirling plume of dust with speeds rarely over 70 mph. These differ from tornadoes in that they are not associated with a thunderstorm (or any cloud) and are usually very weak.

## When are tornadoes most likely to occur?

Tornadoes can happen at any time of the year and at any time of the day. In the southern states, peak tornado season is from March through May. Peak times for tornadoes in the northern states are during the summer. A few southern states have a second peak time for tornado outbreaks in the fall. Tornadoes are most likely to occur between 3 p.m. and 9 p.m.

## Where are tornadoes most likely to occur?

The geography of the central part of the United States, known as the Great Plains, is suited to bring all the ingredients together to forms tornadoes. More than 500 tornadoes typically occur in this area every year and is why it is commonly known as "Tornado Alley". Texas, Oklahoma, Kansas, Nebraska, South Dakota, North Dakota, Iowa, Missouri, Arkansas, and Louisiana.

## BEFORE A TORNADO:

Have a disaster plan. Make sure everyone knows where to go in case a tornado threatens. Make sure you know which county or parish you live in. Prepare a kit with emergency food for your home. Have enough food and water for at least 3 days.

## DURING A TORNADO:

Go to a basement. If you do not have a basement, go to an interior room without windows on the lowest floor such as a bathroom or closet. If you can, get under a sturdy piece of furniture, like a table.

If you live in a mobile home, get out. They offer little protection against tornadoes. Get out of automobiles. Do not try to outrun a tornado in your car, leave it immediately. If you're outside, go to a ditch or low-lying area and lie flat in it. Stay away from fallen power lines and stay out of damaged areas.

## IF YOU'RE IN SCHOOL DURING A TORNADO:

Every school should have a disaster plan and have frequent drills. Basements offer the best protection. Schools without basements should use interior rooms and hallways on the lowest floor away from windows. Crouch down on your knees and protect your head with your arms.

Follow the above-mentioned information and you will do just fine....

# CHAPTER 2

## The History of Hurricanes in Puerto Rico

Juracán is the phonetic name given by the Spanish colonizers to the zemi or God of turmoil and disorder which the Taíno natives in Puerto Rico, Hispaniola, Jamaica, and Cuba, as well as the Island Caribs and Arawak natives elsewhere in the Caribbean, believed controlled the weather, particularly hurricanes, the latter word derives from the idol's name.

The word "juracán" merely represented the storms per se, which according to Taíno mythology were deposited and controlled by the goddess Guabancex, also known as the one whose fury destroys everything.

The Taínos were aware of the spiraling wind pattern of hurricanes. They had knowledge on how to survive any storm way before the Spaniards set foot on the island.

The Taínos used their magical powers that were transmitted from their God. The zemi idol was said to portray a woman, but the most common depiction of Guabancex presents a furious face with her arms extended in a pattern.

According to Taíno mythology, the zemi of Guabancex was entrusted to the ruler of a mystical land, Aumatex. This granted her the title of Cacique of the Wind, but it also imposed the responsibility of repeatedly appeasing the goddess throughout his long reign.

Furthermore, due to the importance of the wind for travel between island and the need of mild weather imperative for a successful crop, other caciques would offer her part of their food during the Chohoba ceremony. However, given Guabancex's unpredictable temper, these efforts often failed.

When they did, she would leave his domain enraged and with the intent of bringing destruction to all in her path, unleashing the "juracán". She began by interrupting the balance established by Boinayel and Marohu, the idols of rain and drought.

By rotating her arms in a spiral, Guabancex would pick the water of the ocean and land, placing it under the command of Coatrisquie who violently forced it back over the Taíno settlements destroying their bohios and crops. She would threaten the other idols to have them join the chaos. She was always preceded by Guayaba, who signaled her eventual arrival with clouds, lightning, and thunder.

The eastern and most of the Greater Antilles, Puerto Rico is often in the path of the North Atlantic tropical storms and hurricanes which tend to come ashore on the east coast.

The Taíno believed that upon reaching the rainforest peak of El Yanique, the goddess and her associates would clash with their supreme divinity, Yúcahu, who was believed to live there.

Guabancex has an unspecified connection to Caorao, an idol that was also associated with storms and that was said to bring them forth by playing the cobo, a musical instrument made from a marine seashell.

## The history of hurricanes in Puerto Rico starts with the arrival of Christopher Columbus to the island on November 19, 1493.

Even though the island was discovered that year, the first Spanish settlement in Puerto Rico was established years later by Juan Ponce de León. This is the reason for having the first official records of tropical cyclones passing through Puerto Rico in the first decade of the 1500s. From that time there are records of tropical cyclones in Puerto Rico until the present times.

The naming system of storms was based on the catholic tradition of naming the storm with the saint of the day. There was also the case that storms repeated in the same day on different years such as with San Felipe I and San Felipe II on September 13th, 1876, and 1928, respectively.

This tradition of naming storms that way ended with hurricane Betsy in 1956 which is still remembered. In Puerto Rico, as Santa Clara.

Years later with the passage of hurricane Donna in 1960, the storm was recognized as San Lorenzo.

Before I continue with the stories that occurred during the hurricanes, I want to take you back in time so that you may understand the hurricane season in the Caribbean.

Let us look at the 16th Century. There were plenty of tropical storms that were documented.

The first tropical hurricane documented in Puerto Rico was "San Roque" on August 16, 1508. It was reported by Juan Ponce de León. His ship was brought to the shore by the high winds and waves in the southwest coast of Puerto Rico. The southwest area was the most affected.

There were a couple of unnamed Tropical Storms during 1513, 1514, or 1515. Historians in recent times have been leaning more towards 1514 as the date.

Lots of Indians died due to the plagues and lack of food. In the "West Indies Documents." There are also reports of the treasurer of Puerto Rico. All the damage by the storm in Puerto Rico were reported to the Crown in Spain.

On October 4-5. 1526, hurricane San Francisco was documented as a violent hurricane that moved slowly over the north of Puerto Rico. It also affected the Dominican Republic on October 5. This hurricane caused extensive damage and widespread flooding.

Hurricane "Santa Ana" on July 26. 1530, was the first of three tropical cyclones that affected Puerto Rico that year. Some historians documented of five tropical cyclones that year, but two of them are doubtful.

This storm affected the entire island and destroyed half of the houses in San Juan. Some historians guessed that the storm passed in July 28.

Puerto Rico had a population of 3,100 inhabitants based on that year's census.

Tropical Storm "San Hipólito", on August 22, 1530, affected the entire island with extensive flooding and a lot of crop damage.

Hurricane San Ramón was a violent hurricane that caused extensive flooding and crop damage on August 31, 1530. There was so much suffering that many of the residents considered leaving the island.

There was unnamed Tropical Storms in July or August 1537.

Some historians spoke of three tropical cyclones that year. Due the lack of evidence, only one can be attributed. The storm caused extensive damage to agriculture and widespread flooding. Many deaths were attributed to the storm, especially of slaves.

On September 7, 1545, there was an unnamed hurricane. This hurricane was reported by visual witness in the Dominican Republic. It is presumed that it affected Puerto Rico. Apparently, it was a large slow-moving storm that caused a lot of rain but was not very intense in terms of winds.

Based on historian Alejandro Tapia, Hurricane "San Bartolomé was the first tropical cyclone designated with the saint of the day. The earlier tropical cyclones were designated by historians' years later after their passages. This was a severe hurricane that caused widespread damage in San Juan and in Santo Domingo on August 24-25 1568...

September 12, 1575, Tropical Storm "San Mateo" was the last tropical hurricane in Puerto Rico in the 16th Century. It was the first of five to occur in the Saint Mathew's Day, "Día de San Mateo". There are no details about its effects and trajectory.

The 17th Century was the time that had almost no cyclones reported. It is believed that there is the assumption that some were not reported due to the lack of communication.

The big crisis of abandon and lack of communication with the other Spanish colonies and Spain that the island suffered during this century. This crisis left the island basically drifting in a social and economic stall. These effects were felt directly in the records of hurricanes in that time because little or no information was every time found due to the lack of reports of every kind in that period.

Hurricane "San Leoncio" occurred on September 12, 1615. It was a severe hurricane that caused extensive damage to the San Juan Cathedral, agriculture specially the sugar crops. There were several deaths. In San Juan harbor, some ships with cargo sank.

Due to the lack of food in the island, a lot of it had to be imported from the neighboring islands. This was the first tropical cyclone to hit the island since "San Mateo" 40 years earlier.

Tropical Storm "San Nicomedes" passed through the northern coast of the island on September 15, 1626. It caused close to thirty deaths. In San Juan Bay, thirty ships were sunken.

Based on reports, there were unnamed hurricanes in September 1642. It was documented that a severe hurricane of big size and strength hit the island. The day of passage is unknown and because of that the storm has no name. It destroyed houses and affected the agriculture. Years earlier, the cacao was beginning to be cultivated, but it was badly affected.

Unknown day of a hurricane that hit the island on august 1657, Caused big damage to the agriculture which caused lack of food. It ended destroying the cacao crops which were abandoned because no one took care of them later. Some historians say that from 1657 until the end of the century there were other cyclones in Puerto Rico, but the evidence is not very clear.

## The18th Century

This Century is much more active in terms of tropical cyclones in Puerto Rico because the reports are completer and more frequent.

Let's begin with Hurricane "San Zacarias" which hit Puerto Rico on September 6, 1713. Fifty-six years has passed since the last cyclone. It caused a big storm surge on the south coast, and it is estimated that a lot of damage was cause on the south side of the island.

Tropical Storm "San Candido" was documented on October 3, 1713.It occurred four weeks after the last storm. Hurricane "San Cándido" passed close to the south part of the island. It also affected the Dominican Republic. The storm caused a lot of damage in the south coast.

Tropical Tempest "Santa Regina" passed over Puerto Rico on September 7, 1718. It went near the northeast side of the island. It caused some damage in San Juan. The "Nuns Convent" in San Juan was damaged badly. It lost its roof.

Tropical Storm "Santa Rosa" passed to the south of the island on August 30, 1730. There has been not much information on this storm. The only thing documented was that it passed causing damage to plantations and houses.

## Hurricane "Santa Rosa" August 30, 1738

Exactly eight years after the last storm occurred a tropical cyclone with the same name but with hurricane strength at this time. It Caused extensive damage to house and agriculture.

San Juan was badly affected. It is estimated that it entered in the eastern side of the island, crossing it and later affecting the Dominican Republic.

## September 12, 1738 Hurricane "San Leoncio"

The route of this storm was interesting as it entered the Caribbean Sea by Guadeloupe then moving west-northwest close to St. Thomas and changing west over the south side of Puerto Rico then to the south of Hispaniola on September 13th. Caused a lot of flooding in the south side of the island affecting agriculture, San Juan did not report much damage.

## August 3, 1740 Hurricane "San Esteban"

This hurricane passed close to the south of the island then later affecting the northeast of the Dominican Republic. The city of Ponce reported the most damage.

## September 1, 1740 Hurricane "San Vicente"

Second hurricane of that year in Puerto Rico. Affected San Juan and the northern side of the island, apparently it was not a strong hurricane.

## October 28, 1742 Hurricane "San Judas Tadeo"

Passed at some distance north of the island after affecting St. Thomas and turning more west-northwest. Strong south winds caused high seas in the south coast of Puerto Rico causing damage to some English ships. This resulted in the occupation by some of the locals of one of the ships that was brought onshore by the storm.

### August 18, 1751 Tropical Storm "San Agapito"

The storm affected the entire island, and it is possible that the route was across the island from south to north. An earthquake was reported during the passage of the storm.

### September 19, 1766 Hurricane "San Genaro"

Severe hurricane that affected the east half of the island. Caused damage to rice, corn, bananas, coconuts, and other crops. The trajectory of this storm is very doubtful as it passed over Monserrat on September 13th possibly turning after that passing over northeast Puerto Rico 6 days later, which is too much time.

### October 7-8, 1766 Hurricane "San Marcos"

Passed over Guadeloupe were a storm surge combined with a river overflow created a big flooding. Crossed Puerto Rico from southeast to northwest causing the worst damage in the east side even though it affected the entire island.

### August 7, 1767 Hurricane "San Cayetano"

Passed somewhat retired from the south of the island. Caused big flooding and damage to crops. In the island of Martinique 1,600 people were drowned.

### August 28, 1772 Hurricane "San Agustín"

It was a strong hurricane that passed through the Leeward Islands, then St. Thomas, crossing Puerto Rico from Fajardo to Mayaguez and affecting Hispaniola. Damage in Puerto Rico was severe.

### August 31,1777 Hurricane "San Ramón"

Second hurricane of the year passed only three days after the last hurricane. Affected the island of Barbados then moving northwest towards the Leeward Islands and St. Thomas passing over the northeast side of Puerto Rico with lesser damage than the earlier storm.

"Saint Peter" passed close to the southwest corner of the island then over the Dominican Republic. Its effects are unknown.

## June 13, 1780 Tropical Storm "San Antonio"

Only cyclone on record in the month of June in Puerto Rico. Passed close or just south of Puerto Rico then over the Dominican Republic. Damaged an English ship in the south coast. Affected crops and properties in Puerto Rico causing a lot of damage in the Dominican Republic.

## October 14, 1780 Hurricane "San Calixto"

Known as the "Great Antilles Hurricane" is one of the most infamous and damaging of all times. The hurricane dismantled Barbados with winds estimated in close to 200mph destroying trees completely until flying. In St. Lucia it caused 6,000 deaths and in Martinique it caused 9,000 deaths in part due to the storm surge.

The center of the hurricane passed close to the southwest tip of Puerto Rico then over the east side of the Dominican Republic turning towards Bermuda where it sank 50 ships.

Damage in Puerto Rico was not very important, but this storm was included in the list due to the importance of the damage it caused. Affected severely St. Vincent and Grenada.

## September 25, 1785 Tropical Storm "San Lupo"

Passed over Puerto Rico causing severe damage, in the rural areas. For the first time a governor, Juan Dabán visited the island to offer relief and inspect the damage.

## August 16, 1788 Hurricane "San Roque"

Hurricane that passed south of the island but due to its large size affected it entirely. This was the last tropical cyclone of the 18th Century in Puerto Rico and by this time the island had 35 localities and population of 100,000 people.

# 19 Century

## September 4, 1804 Hurricane "Santa Rosalía"

First hurricane to affect Puerto Rico in the 19th Century. It passed north of the island without much important damage. Later the storm affected extremely hard the city of Charleston, South Carolina.

Hurricane "San Vicente" passed south of Puerto Rico in September 11,1806. It caused a lot of damage in Ponce. It also affected severely Dominica causing one hundred and thirty-one deaths.

Hurricane "San Jacinto" crossed Puerto Rico from southeast to northwest on August 17 thru the 19, 1807.

It was a very slow-moving storm that affected the island for fifty hours. This hurricane flooded all the rivers and destroyed much of the crops. There were many lives loss. Before reaching Puerto Rico, the storm moved over the Leeward Islands then over the Virgin Islands. After destroying Puerto Rico, it went to the Dominican Republic.

Tropical Storm "San Liborio" caused a lot of damage in the southwest part of the island on July 23rd; 1813. The coffee crops were hit severely.

## August 21, 1813 Tropical Storm "Santa Juana"

Affected Dominica before passing close to the south of Puerto Rico, then the storm affected South Carolina. Damage to agriculture July 23, 1814, Tropical Storm "San Liborio"

One year after, the same day another tropical cyclone passed close to Puerto Rico. Again, the storm affected hard the south side and it was felt in San Juan. At the time the storm passed there was a 7-month drought, but the passage was not very helpful because it destroyed the crops.

## September 18-20, 1816 Huracane "San José de Cupertino"

Passed over Martinique and then close or over the south coast of Puerto Rico. Damage to crops.

## September 22, 1818 Tropical Storm "San Mauricio"

Cause minor damage to the island. The passage of this storm is unclear, it is reported that it was felt in the south side of the island, especially in Guayama.

On September 21-22, 1819, Hurricane "San Mateo" moved over the Virgin Island causing 101 deaths. Then it went to Puerto Rico on the night of September 21st. The storm sank a lot of ships in San Juan. It was a very severe hurricane. It was estimated that this hurricane destroyed most of the houses and crops in Puerto Rico.

Hurricane "San Pedro" passed through Puerto Rico on September 9-10, 1824; very close to the south coast affecting mainly the area from Juana Díaz to Cabo Rojo.

## Hurricane "Santa Ana" hit the island on July 26-27, 1825.

Santa Ana is one of the strongest hurricanes in record in Puerto Rico. It caused 374 deaths and 1,200 injured.

It made landfall in Puerto Rico at 11pm in Humacao and Yabucoa leaving the island by Arecibo and Vega Baja at 8:30am. The storm affected mainly the east, north and center of the island. The southwest was not much affected.

## This is the second storm to cause more deaths in Puerto Rico's history only after "San Ciriaco" in 1899

In San Juan the tempest destroyed the poor suburbs leaving the city without communication to the rest of the island. Apparently, the hurricane was small. If it were a larger the storm, it would have destroyed the entire island.

Guadeloupe measured a pressure of 27.10 inches of mercury or 918 millibars. The storm's intensity in Puerto Rico is estimated to be around category 4 force with winds of around 150mph.

In the harbors around the island, some ships were sunk.

## August 17, 1827 Tropical Storm "San Jacinto"

Crossed the island from southeast to north affecting the agriculture

## August 13, 1835 Hurricane "San Hipólito"

Crossed the island from southeast to north lasting around 6 to 7 hours over land affecting mainly the east and north of the island. This storm passed north of Hispaniola, over Cuba and affected Galveston, Texas.

## 1837, August 2nd-3rd Hurricane "Nuestra Señora de los Angeles"

It was a severe hurricane that crossed the island from southeast to north in a period of 10 to 12 hours. The first storm to have a barometric reading in Puerto Rico were San Juan got a minimal pressure of 28.00 inches of mercury or 948 millibars. In San Juan the storm killed 11 people and sank some ships.

## August 18, 1851 Hurricane "San Agapito"

Passed very close to the southwest side of the island but the effects took all of Puerto Rico. The storm was estimated to have winds of around 100 mph sustained when the closest point of approach 1. Big damage to agriculture. The storm entered Florida by the city of Apalachicola on August 22nd.

## September 5, 1852 Hurricane "San Lorenzo"

The storm made landfall in southwest Puerto Rico with winds estimated in 70 mph to 80 mph 1. Affected the southwest side of Puerto Rico causing big flooding and damage to Guayanilla and Mayaguez.

## October 29, 1852 Hurricane "San Narciso"

One of the strong hurricanes of Puerto Rico's history affected the entire island. Caused 211 deaths because of the flooding. The storm passed directly over St. Thomas the afternoon of October 29th with estimated sustained winds of 120 mph and a reported pressure of 952 millibars 1 causing 600 deaths by drowning and in the bay 50 ships sunk.

The storm made landfall in Puerto Rico at around 5-6 pm somewhat weaker than when it hit St. Thomas passing over Caguas and leaving the island in the west.

The rare thing with this storm is that with such insignificant pressure readings, 29.60 in/hg or 1002 mb in San Juan and 29.40 in/hg or 995 mb in Arroyo, the storm caused so much damage. The first tropical cyclone where the wind speed is known.

## August 21, 1871 Hurricane "Santa Juana"

This is the first tropical cyclone in which Puerto Rico got the warning of the storm coming because the telegraph and the ultramarine cable was already working in the Caribbean. The storm passed over the Virgin Islands and a message was sent to San Juan.

The eye of the hurricane moved over the Virgin Island and around 20 miles northeast of Puerto Rico with estimated sustained winds of 120 mph 1.St. Thomas got a pressure of 28.40 in/hg or 962 millibars and 27 deaths. The storm passed just north of San Juan with a pressure measured of 29.53 in/hg or 1000 millibars. Damage in Puerto Rico was minimal.

## September 13, 1876 Hurricane "San Felipe I"

One of the worst hurricanes in the 19th century affected the island by 10 hours crossing it from east to west. The storm made landfall with estimated sustained winds of 100 mph weakening and with a pressure report from Mayaguez of 991 millibars 1. San Juan got winds of 60mph and a pressure of 29.20 in/hg or 988 millibars and a rain total of 4.71 inches.

This is the first storm were rain was measured in Puerto Rico. A total of 19 deaths was associated to the storm, by this time the first daily weather observations were done in Puerto Rico.

## November 28, 1878 Tropical Storm "San Rufo"

First tropical cyclone to affect Puerto Rico in the month of November. The storm passed just over the south coast of Puerto Rico in a just south of due west direction with estimated sustained winds of 70 mph

1. The storm was felt in the east and south of the island with San Juan reporting winds of 20mph and a pressure of 29.64 in/hg, 1004mb. There was little damage reported.

## September 1-2, 1888 Hurricane "San Gil"

Passed some 100 to 150 nm north of Puerto Rico estimated as a category 1 hurricane 1. The effects in the island were the heavy rains which caused over 100 deaths due to river flooding. This hurricane is like Donna in 1960 which had the same tragic effect in Puerto Rico without passing over the island.

## September 3-4, 1889 Hurricane "San Martín"

Passed near St. Thomas with estimated sustained winds of 105 mph at around 40 nm from the northeast tip of Puerto Rico and at around 90 nm northeast of San Juan 1. Damage to banana crops only. Winds of 48 mph were measured and a pressure of 29.43 in/hg, 996mb, in San Juan and 29.30 in/hg (992mb) in Humacao.

## August 19th-20, 1891 Hurricane "San Magín"

The eye of the hurricane passed close to the southwest tip of Puerto Rico in a west-northwest direction with estimated sustained winds of 100-105 mph 1. Big flooding was reported in the island with the city of Carolina 6 to 8 feet under water. This was one of the deadliest hurricanes in the Antilles were it killed more than 700 people in Martinique.

## 1893, August 16th-17th Hurricane "San Roque"

Entered the island by Patillas at 7-8 pm and left Puerto Rico by 3am in Isabela. The storm was estimated to have sustained winds of 115 mph at time of landfall 1. San Juan got 29.17 in/hg, 987mb, pressure and winds of 55 mph with rains of 2.36 inches. This is the first storm were flags were used to warn people of a storm coming, this was done in the government offices. The hurricane affected hard the railroads.

## 1896, August 31st-September 1st Hurricane "San Ramón"

Last hurricane in Puerto Rico under the Spanish control. Crossed the southwest area of the island making landfall in the vicinity of Ponce with estimated sustained winds of 100 mph.

## August 8, 1899 Hurricane "San Ciriaco"

This hurricane has some records that are hard or impossible to break:

1. The last hurricane of the 19th Century.
2. First hurricane with Puerto Rico under the control of USA.
3. The natural disaster that has killed most people in Puerto Rico's history; 3,369 deaths.
4. The storm that has caused more rain in 24 hours with a total of 23.00 inches in Adjuntas.

5.   First tropical cyclone with a rain map in Puerto Rico and the first under the National Weather Service, NWS, in Puerto Rico.

San Ciriaco formed near the Cape Verde Islands and crossed the Atlantic towards the Antilles, then moved towards the United States turning east over the North Atlantic towards Europe.

The hurricane made landfall in southeast Puerto Rico at around 8am with estimated sustained winds of 140-145 mph and a pressure of 27.75 in/hg or 939 millibars leaving the island around 2pm in the vicinity of Aguadilla 1. The storm's hurricane wind radii was of 80-85 nm and the rain area was of around 385 nm. Pressure in San Juan was of 29.17 in/hg, 987mb, and rain totals of 6.37 inches.

In Mayaguez the winds picked up to 112mph and a pressure of 28.86 in/hg, 977mb.

In 48 hours, an average of 10.1 inches of rain was estimated for the entire island. That is the normal rain rate of 2 summer months in Puerto Rico. During the hurricane a total of 890 people died and 1,294 were drowned. Some injured died later and the total was elevated to 3,369 deaths. Damage estimates to property were a total of $35,889,013 3.

In the article "La marejada ciclónica de San Ciriaco" or "The Storm Surge of San Ciriaco" 2 it is mentioned the deadly storm surge that entered in Humacao near one mile inland in some places with the winds coming from the east, onshore, in the northern eyewall of the storm.

Storm surge estimates are of at least 15 feet in the area which has places like Punta Santiago which are several feet below sea level and were entire families were lost in the storm and were never found after. San Ciriaco was the deadliest storms in Puerto Rico and is also on record as one of the strongest to hit the island and still more than a century after its passage is a storm that deserves to be studied in every aspect.

# CHAPTER 3

## Hurricanes and Tropical Storms in Puerto Rico from 1900 to 1979

### 20th Century

### July 7, 1901 Tropical Storm "San Cirilo"

First storm to hit Puerto Rico in the 20th Century. The center of the storm moved over the southwest tip of Puerto Rico in a northwesterly direction with estimated sustained winds of 70 mph in the early morning of July 7th 1.

The storm was mostly experienced in the southwest area of the island and produced rains of 5 to 6 inches in 72 hours in Barranquitas, Caguas and Humacao. The wind report of San Juan was of 52 mph and a pressure of 29.60 in/hg, 1002 mb).

### September 11-12, 1901 Tropical Storm "San Vicente"

The center of this tropical storm moved over the north coast of Puerto Rico in a westerly direction with estimated sustained winds of 60 mph during the night of September 11th and early morning of September 12th 1. The wind report from San Juan was of 52 mph and a pressure of 29.89 (1012 mb). The storm affected all the crops in Puerto Rico, especially the citrus.

## September 6-7, 1910 Hurricane "San Zacarias"

The eye of this hurricane passed around 20 miles south of the south coast of Puerto Rico in a westerly direction with sustained winds estimated in 100 mph 1. Strong gusts were reported in the northeast side of the island and in San Juan winds reached 72 mph with a pressure of 29.66 in/hg 1004 mb.

The rest of the island apparently did not report very much activity. The rare thing with this hurricane is that the worst conditions were experienced in the northeast side of the island with the storm passing close to the south coast.

## August 11, 1915 Hurricane "San Triburcio"

The storm passed around 100 miles south of Puerto Rico in a westerly direction with winds estimated in 100 mph near the center. Two people were drowned in the sea in Cabo Rojo, the storm caused mountainous seas in the south coast.

Also, the agriculture was affected with crops damaged. The minimal pressure in San Juan was of 29.77 in/hg, 1008 mb, and winds of 62 mph. The strongest winds were experienced in the Central Mountain Range and the south.

## August 22, 1915 Hurricane "San Hipólito"

Estimated to be a small sized hurricane that crossed Puerto Rico from east to west. The storm's intensity was estimated to be at 90 mph sustained at time of landfall and weakening as it crossed the island. San Juan reported winds of 92 mph and a pressure of 29.82 in/hg, 1010 mb. One death was attributed to the storm and the worst damage was reported in the east and northern part of Puerto Rico, especially Santurce. The monetary damage is estimated at $1,000,000 dollars.

## September 9th-10, 1921 Hurricane "San Pedro"

This hurricane passed well south of Puerto Rico in a west-northwesterly direction as a category one storm, then it moved in a northerly direction over eastern Hispaniola re-curving into the open Atlantic passing close to Bermuda. Cabo Rojo, PR had winds of 60 mph and a pressure of 29.68 in/hg, 1005 mb and Ponce reported a pressure of 29.70 in/hg, 1006 mb.

The winds measured in San Juan were of 44 mph with a pressure of 29.82 in/hg, 1010 mb. The main effect of the storm was heavy surf in the south coast and damage was minimal, one death was reported.

## 1926, July 23rd-24, 1926 Hurricane "San Liborio"

The storm entered the Caribbean Sea by Martinique and strengthening as it moved in a general west-northwest heading until making landfall in the southwest of Puerto Rico with estimated sustained winds of 80 mph the night of July 23rd. The winds in San Juan were measured of 66 mph and a pressure of 29.62 in/hg, 1003 mb.

The hurricane killed 25 people and damage estimates are of $5,000,000 dollars. Many houses were destroyed around the island.

## September 13, 1928 Hurricane "San Felipe II"

This is considered one of the most intense hurricanes in the history of the Antilles and the strongest in Puerto Rico's history. This infamous hurricane developed in the Cape Verde Islands reported on September 6th.

Moving generally in a westerly direction for the next few days, the storm strengthened into hurricane intensity and further increasing its force passed over the island of Guadeloupe the afternoon of September 12th with sustained winds estimated to be near 125 mph, 110 kts) and a reported pressure in the island of 940 millibars.

As the storm entered the Caribbean Sea, it continued to strengthen becoming a category 5 intensity, Saffir-Simpson Scale, hurricane.

"San Felipe" made landfall in Southeast Puerto Rico in the vicinity of Guayama-Arroyo at around 2 PM AST September 13th with officially estimated sustained winds of 160 mph and a measured pressure in Arroyo of 27.50 in/hg or 931 millibars. It is not known if this pressure was measured in the eye.

For the next eight to ten hours the eye of the hurricane crossed Puerto Rico from southeast to northwest without losing much strength, still with category 5 intensity when it left the northwest side of the island in the vicinity of Aguadilla at around 10-11 PM AST September 13th.

The wind report from San Juan was of sustained 160 mph at around 1 PM AST before the instrument was destroyed by the winds. Stronger winds were probably felt after the instrument was destroyed; this are the highest sustained winds ever reported in Puerto Rico. As the official intensity estimates are of 160 mph, 140 kts, when the storm hit Puerto Rico, there are estimates of sustained winds in 180-200 mph were the strongest part of the eyewall passed over, which was the southeast coast of the island.

Damage surveys in the aftermath of the storm reveal that there was catastrophic destruction all around Puerto Rico, but that the towns which were directly in the path of the eye and strongest part of the eyewall were literary "blown" out of the map.

This was the case in places like Guayama, Arroyo all the way north to Naguabo and westward. The storm was also very big as estimates are of hurricane conditions in Guayama for 18 hours, 4 am-10 pm September 13th, and San Juan for 12 hours, 4 am-4 pm September 13th. Rain reports were of 29.60 inches of rain in 48 hours.

After blasting Puerto Rico, the hurricane continued in a west-northwesterly direction over the Bahamas Islands as a category 4 storm finally making landfall in the vicinity of West Palm Beach, Florida in the night of September 17th with estimated sustained winds of 150 mph, 130 kts and a measured pressure of 929 millibars.

The storm made catastrophic damage in Florida also causing a storm surge in Lake Okeechobee showing the massive size and power of the storm, at least 1,800 deaths were caused by the storm in that state.

The storm moved further inland into Florida and the eastern side of the United States while finally dissipating near the Great Lakes area on September 20th.

As mentioned above, Puerto Rico was devastated by the storm and the towns were the eye passed directly over were the worst affected with many places becoming unrecognizable after the event.

At least 312 deaths were related to the hurricane. Damage estimates are of $50,000,000 dollars, which for that time is a very high amount.

A total of 24,728 houses were destroyed and 192,444 were severely affected. Almost no building in Puerto Rico survived the hurricane without any damage 2.

Many sugar cane factories which were new at that time and were valued at millions of dollars were reduced to wreckage by the hurricane. The coffee crops were all lost, and coffee was imported to Puerto Rico from 1929 to 1934 to satisfy local demand 3.

The economy of Puerto Rico which was struggling before the hurricane was further affected by it and it took more than a decade to recuperate entirely from the effects of this infamous storm which to the date, is the strongest hurricane to hit Puerto Rico in its history.

## September 10th-11, 1931 Hurricane "San Nicolás"

Category 1 hurricane that crossed the north coast of Puerto Rico from east to west with estimated sustained winds of 90 mph. The storm made landfall in Fajardo at 8 PM leaving the island by Aguadilla at 2 AM. The hurricane continued in a westward track across the south of Hispaniola and into Yucatan and Mainland Mexico.

The winds in San Juan reached 90 mph from the northwest and a pressure of 29.17 in/hg, 987.8 millibars, at 10 PM AST.

The hurricane lasted around 2 hours in San Juan. Two people died in the storm and the worst damage was to agriculture, estimates are of $200,000 dollars.

Only four years after hurricane "San Felipe" another major storm hits Puerto Rico. "San Ciprián" On September 26-27, 1932. It developed east of the Northern Leeward Islands and strengthened fast becoming a hurricane and crossing St. Marteen, Anguilla and the Virgin Islands as a category 3 hurricane the day of September 26th.

The eye of the hurricane made landfall in Eastern Puerto Rico around PM AST September 26, 1932. It crossed the island during the next 7 hours until leaving Puerto Rico near Mayaguez at 5 AM AST September 27, 1932.

The winds at time of landfall in Puerto Rico were estimated to be of sustained 120 mph or category 3 intensity. There is a pressure report from two ships in Ensenada Honda, Ceiba (landfall point of the hurricane) which measured 27.70 in/hg (938 millibars) and 28.00 in/hg (948 millibars). These pressure reports support at least a category 3 intensity hurricane at landfall in Puerto Rico.

In San Juan, the anemometer broke when the winds reached 66 mph, and they reported a pressure of 980 millibars when the eye of the hurricane passed to their south at around 1 AM AST September 27, 1932.

After affecting Puerto Rico, the hurricane continued in a westward motion across the south coast of Hispaniola and weakening to tropical storm status finally dissipating over Mexico on October 3rd.

Damage in Puerto Rico was extensive across the island and 225 people died because of the storm, damage estimates are of $30,000,000 dollars. Many of the deaths were caused by the collapse of buildings or flying debris.

A total of 25,000 people lost their homes, and 46 municipalities were severely damaged. In the agriculture, the citruses were the worst damaged because they were in the worst affected area. In Arecibo a total of 24 people died when they took shelter in a building that collapsed during the hurricane. Puerto Rico was still recuperating from "San Felipe" and this storm brought more misery and desolation to the island.

## On October 14, 1943, Hurricane "San Calixto" paid us a visit.

This hurricane passed far south of Puerto Rico in a westerly direction. Suddenly, the storm turned in a northward direction passing 70 miles west of Puerto Rico and near Punta Cana, Dominican Republic as a category 1 hurricane, 90 mph.

The storm ended in Nova Scotia. Winds of 60 mph were reported in the west of Puerto Rico, this caused damage to the houses from Cabo Rojo to Aguadilla.

Rains of 12 to 18 inches caused flooding in the rest of the island. No deaths were reported, for first time the Reconnaissance Aircrafts to study the cyclone.

## September 21, 1949 Hurricane "San Mateo"

Short-lived hurricane that passed some 40-60 nm south of Puerto Rico with winds estimated of 80 mph near the center.

In Saint Croix the damage was strong but the effects in Puerto Rico were relatively minor, mainly in the south and southwest side. In Ramey

AFB, Aguadilla winds of 64 mph were measured and in San Juan the winds reached 38 mph. almost all the rivers flooded.

## August 12, 1956, Hurricane Betsy, Santa Clara

Hurricane Betsy developed from a tropical wave on August 9th east of the Lesser Antilles. The storm rapidly strengthened reaching hurricane status reaching an estimated peak of intensity of sustained 120mph, 105 kts winds and weakening before passing over the island of Dominica and very near the southwest of Guadeloupe in the afternoon of August 11th.

At this time, the storm was estimated to have winds of 90 to 110 mph. The hurricane continued moving straight to Puerto Rico making landfall in the southeast of the island by the town of Patillas at 8 AM AST August 12th.

The intensity of the hurricane at this time was estimated to be at 90 mph and the storm was moving at a fast forward speed of 21 mph with an eye of 14 nm in diameter.

In only 3 hours, the eye of the hurricane crossed Puerto Rico leaving the island by Arecibo, north coast, at 11 AM AST August 12th. San Juan reported winds of 92 mph, a pressure of 29.56 in/hg, 1001 mb and rain totals of 3.19 inches.

Ramey Air Force Base, in Aguadilla, reported sustained winds of 85 mph with a gust of 115 mph. The highest rainfall report was in Rio Grande with 8.70 inches.

After passing over Puerto Rico, Betsy continued in a northwest track strengthening back to category 2 intensity and re-curving northeastward into the open waters of the Atlantic losing its tropical characteristics as it moved into cooler waters by the 20th of August.

Damage made by "Santa Clara" in Puerto Rico was bad in the southeast, central, and northern areas of the island, the hurricane did not impact very much the southwest side.

A total of 16 people died in the storm and 15,000 houses were destroyed. Damage estimates are of $40,000,000 dollars. This is the first hurricane that was tracked in radar as it crossed Puerto Rico.

## September 5, 1960 Hurricane Donna, San Lorenzo

Hurricane Donna is one of the infamous Atlantic hurricanes due to the path of destruction the storm left from the Caribbean trough the Bahamas, Florida, and the Eastern Seaboard of the United States.

In Puerto Rico, the effects of Donna were associated with deadly flashfloods which killed over 100 people when the storm passed 70 nm northeast of the island. Donna originated from a tropical wave which became a tropical depression south of the Cape Verde Islands on August 29th.

Moving in a classic, Cape Verde track the depression became a tropical storm on August 30th as it was approaching the Lesser Antilles. Tropical storm Donna became a hurricane on September 1st and still intensifying until reaching its peak of intensity of 160mph, 140 kts, sustained winds when the storm was about 100 nm east-northeast of Guadeloupe on August 4th.

Hurricane Donna weakened somewhat before passing very close to Antigua and near of over Barbuda, St. Marteen, and Anguilla, by this time the hurricane was estimated to have winds of 150 mph when it hit Antigua and Barbuda weakening steadily to 130-135 mph when it passed the St. Marteen area.

Donna continued in a west-northwest track passing close to the north of the Virgin Islands, 36 nm north of St. Thomas and 70 nm northeast of Fajardo, Puerto Rico the afternoon of September 5th with winds estimated to be at 125-130 mph near the center.

The hurricane then moved in a more westward track across the Bahamas blasting the island as a category 4 storm estimated to have winds of 150 mph at that time.

After that, the hurricane made landfall in the Middle Florida Keys in the early morning hours of September 10th with winds of 140 mph and a pressure of 932 millibars.

Then, the hurricane started to recurve over the state making a second landfall near Napes, Florida still as a category 4 intensity hurricane emerging near the city of Daytona as a borderline category 3-4 hurricane and making two more landfalls in the North Carolina Outer Banks and Long Island, New York as a category 2 hurricane.

After that, the hurricane lost its tropical characteristics dissipating over Eastern Canada on September 14th.

Damage in Puerto Rico was mainly due to rain, not much wind was experienced in the island. Rainfall amounts were tremendous with estimates of 15 to 20 inches of rain in a 6-to-10-hour period, which can be a record for Puerto Rico.

These excessive rainfall amounts caused all rivers to flood over their banks killing 107 people by drowning. The worst floods occurred in the eastern half of the island with much of the deaths registered in the city of Humacao were the river claimed most of the lives.

The Red Cross reported 137 people death or missing, 519 destroyed houses and 3,762 houses affected. Many people did not take precautions even with the warnings issued resulting in the tragedy in Humacao were people who did not abandoned their houses and when the river came and swept away their houses, with them inside.

As well as in Puerto Rico, the Leeward Islands, Bahamas, and United States suffered heavy damage by this powerful hurricane.

In Florida, the Keys were blasted by the full force of the winds and storm surge of the hurricane with many islands under the water during the height of the storm. The damage path continued across the Florida Peninsula and the Eastern Seaboard all the way up to New York City and Boston.

## October 2nd-3rd 1961 Tropical Storm Frances

Tropical storm Frances developed just east of the Lesser Antilles on September 30th passing just southwest of Puerto Rico in the night of October 2nd and morning of October 3rd. Heavy rains were reported in the southwest of the island and winds of 35 mph reported.

The storm was estimated to have winds of 60 mph at closest point of approach. Frances the strengthened to hurricane intensity re-curving into the Atlantic and dissipating on October 10th. No deaths associated to the storm in Puerto Rico.

## September 26 1963 Hurricane Edith

This hurricane formed just east of the Lesser Antilles on September 23rd and intensifying until passing Near St. Lucia as a category 2 intensity hurricane.

After weakening the hurricane passed around 20 miles southwest of Puerto Rico with winds of 75 mph night of September 26th. Edith then hit the Dominican Republic and dissipated over the Bahamas on September 29th. The hurricane caused some damage to bridges and crops in the south of Puerto Rico.

## August 23, 1964 Hurricane Cleo

Hurricane Cleo formed east of the Lesser Antilles moving in a westward track on August 20th. During the next few days, the storm strengthened until reaching hurricane intensity and blasting Guadeloupe with winds of 130-135 mph sustained on August 22nd.

After that, Cleo continued in a westward track passing 100 nm south of Puerto Rico with winds of 155 mph causing minor damage and with winds of 52 mph reported in Punta Tuna, Maunabo.

The hurricane passed just south of Barahona, Dominican Republic and over southwestern Haiti as a category 4 hurricane, weakening and crossing Eastern Cuba the eye of Cleo moved over South Florida as a rapidly strengthening category 2 hurricane with winds of 105 mph and a pressure of 968 millibars. The Cleo re-curved inland over the North Carolina area and moved out into the ocean were it regained hurricane intensity finally dissipating east of Nova Scotia on September 5th.

## August 26, 1966 Hurricane Faith

Hurricane Faith developed east of the Lesser Antilles on August 21st and moving in a general westward direction and intensifying until becoming a hurricane.

Faith passed around 90 nm north of San Juan moving west-northwest with winds of 85 mph near the center. Wind reports in San Juan were of 45 mph and minimal damage. The hurricane caused high seas in the north coast. After that, the hurricane re-curved after reaching the peak intensity of 125mph.

## September 28, 1966 Hurricane Inez

Inez was a powerful hurricane that passed around 70 nm south of Puerto Rico on September 28th. The winds at that time were estimated to be of 150 mph sustained near the center.

Inez developed east of the Antilles on September 21st and moved towards the islands until reaching Guadeloupe on September 27th, the storm was estimated to have winds of 125 mph when it hit the island.

Inez continued to strengthen as it moved south of Puerto Rico and over Southern Hispaniola, then having a very erratic track over Cuba, South Florida, Yucatan and finally Mainland Mexico on October 11th. A reconnaissance aircraft measured a wind of 197 mph at 4,000 feet when the storm was south of Puerto Rico.

At that time, it was the record of speed for cyclones in the area. In Puerto Rico the highest winds were of 52 mph in Tallaboa, Peñuelas and in Mona Island the winds were estimated in the 70-80 mph range. Damage was minimal in Puerto Rico.

## September 9, 1967 Hurricane Beulah

Powerful category 4 hurricane that passed some 40 miles to the southwest of Puerto Rico with winds estimated of 145 mph near the center. Beulah formed east of the Antilles on September 5th and moved over the St. Lucia area as a tropical storm, then the storm rapidly strengthened to hurricane intensity and reaching major hurricane status south of Puerto Rico.

The hurricane made a sharp turn to the left passing just south of Hispaniola and weakening fast, then the hurricane hit Yucatan as a category 2 storm and making a final landfall in the Brownsville, Texas area as a category 3 intensity hurricane, finally dissipating inland on September 22nd.

Damage in Puerto Rico was in the south coast, to beach houses, boats, and roads.

## September 15th-16, 1975 Tropical Storm Eloise

Eloise passed 30 to 40 nm north of Puerto Rico as a tropical storm moving in a westward direction.

Eloise became a tropical depression on September 13th and maintaining that strength as it moved over the extreme Northern Leeward Islands. When it passed north of Puerto Rico the system reached tropical storm status and it was estimated to have winds of 50 mph as it moved north of the island.

Then, the storm briefly reached hurricane intensity making landfall in the Puerto Plata, Dominican Republic area on September 17th with winds estimated to be at 75 mph.

Eloise ended making landfall in the Florida Panhandle on September 23rd with winds of 125 mph, 110kts, and a pressure of 955 millibars. This resulted in very extensive wind and storm surge damage in the area and an outbreak of tornadoes associated with the storm.

In Puerto Rico, the damage was caused by very heavy rainfall and extensive flooding around the island. The southwest side was the worst affected and 44 people died by drowning.

Rainfall data indicates that the record of 23 inches of rain in 24 hours by hurricane "San Ciriaco" in 1899 may have been exceeded but the information cannot be confirmed.

# CHAPTER 4

# Tropical Storm Claudette

Claudette was a weak tropical storm that passed over the north coast of Puerto Rico in a westward direction. Apparently, the storm weakened to tropical depression strength just before landfall.

Claudette never got very much strength and ended making landfall near Corpus Christy, Texas on July 24th. The winds were estimated to be around 50 mph, the storm brought a lot of rain to the area because damage estimates are of $609 million dollars. Damage in Puerto Rico was minimal.

## August 30, 1979 Hurricane David

Hurricane David originated from a tropical wave that emerged from the west coast of Africa becoming a tropical depression on August 25th east of the Windward Islands.

Moving in a westward direction, the system continued to organize and became a tropical storm and later a hurricane as it was getting closer to the islands.

David became a powerful category 4 hurricane as it blasted through the islands of Martinique and Dominica with sustained winds of 145 mph and a pressure of 933 millibars the afternoon of August 29th.

This resulted in massive destruction in those islands. David continued moving west-northwestward passing around 70 nm southwest of Puerto Rico with an amazing intensity of 175 mph sustained winds and a pressure of 924 millibars.

David weakened slightly and re-strengthened just prior to landfall near Santo Domingo, Dominican Republic with estimated sustained winds of 175 mph and a pressure of 926 millibars in the afternoon of August 31st.

David is one of the worst hurricanes in the Dominican Republic's history, damage was catastrophic and more than 1,200 people died and many others were left homeless and in the misery.

The high mountains of Hispaniola almost killed David from a powerful category 5 hurricane to a tropical storm when it left the island by the coast of Haiti, and skimming Cuba.

David passed just east of Miami in a northward direction as a category 1 hurricane and strengthened to 100 mph moving along the coast from West Palm Beach all the way to the Georgia-South Carolina border as a category 1 hurricane. David ended losing its tropical characteristics on September 8th.

David is one of the worst hurricanes to hit the Caribbean in the 20th Century. When the hurricane passed south of Puerto Rico, hurricane conditions were experienced in the southeast, south, and southwest areas of the island with estimated sustained winds of 75-85 mph.

The rest of the island experienced tropical storm winds gusting to hurricane force at times. The seas became extremely violent in the south coast of the island and flooding was severe across the island, especially in the north coast. A total of 7 people died during the storm. David was followed by tropical storm Frederick 5 days later.

## September 4 1979 Tropical Storm Frederick

Only 5 days after David, tropical storm Frederick passed directly over Puerto Rico. Frederick developed east of the Antilles on August 29th following the track of David. Becoming a hurricane east of the Leeward Islands, Frederick found some strong upper-level wind shear due to the outflow of hurricane David.

The weak storm crossed Puerto Rico from east to west with winds of 50 mph and a pressure of 1004 millibars.

After passing over Puerto Rico, Frederick affected the Dominican Republic, Haiti, Cuba and entering the Gulf of Mexico where it became a powerful category4 hurricane.

Frederick ended making landfall in the Mississippi-Alabama coasts with sustained winds of 135 mph and a pressure of 946 millibars in the night of September 13th.

Damage to the area was very heavy and estimates are of $3.5 billion dollars in damage, one of the most expensive hurricanes of all times in the United States. In Puerto Rico the damage was caused by flooding and damage estimates cannot be separated between David and Frederick and are a total of $125 million dollars.

The center of this fast-moving tropical storm moved through Puerto Rico from the southeast to the north-central coast of the island in a period of less than three hours.

The storm's intensity was of sustained 60 mph at time of landfall. In San Juan the wind report was of 40 mph with a pressure of 29.66 in/hg or 1004 millibars. Rainfall amounts of 2-3 inches were reported. The strongest winds in Puerto Rico were reported in Fajardo with sustained 50 mph and a gust to 60 mph. Damage was minimal.

## November 7, 1964 Tropical Storm Klaus

Second storm in Puerto Rico's history in the month of November and is often remembered by the fact that it hit the island in the election's day of 1984. The system developed south of Puerto Rico in the Caribbean Sea on November 5th, moving northeastward, and strengthening to tropical storm intensity the center of the storm passed just east extreme Eastern Puerto Rico during the night of the 7th.

The storm's intensity was of around 50 to 60 mph, but the area of strongest winds remained offshore Puerto Rico and over the US Virgin Islands.

After affecting the area, the storm intensified to hurricane status in the 8th while moving over the Atlantic Ocean and thereafter losing tropical characteristics in the 13th.

Damage in Puerto Rico was relatively minor with highest winds reported in Roosevelt Roads with gusts to 37 mph. Rainfall amounts peaked at 3 inches. Trees down and power lines affected were the biggest results, other than disrupting somewhat the election process.

## 1989, September 18th; Hurricane Hugo:
## 1995, September 5th-6th; Hurricane Luis:

Hurricane Luis was a powerful category 4 hurricane that originated in the far Eastern Atlantic Ocean and blasted the Northern Leeward Islands with winds of up to 135 mph bringing tropical storm conditions to Puerto Rico.

Luis formed from an organized tropical wave that emerged off the west coast of Africa and moved into the Atlantic Ocean, the first warning was issued by the National Hurricane Center the morning of August 27th. The system steadily intensified as it moved westward over the open Atlantic during the next several days and became a hurricane during the day of August 30th.

A very strong mid-level to surface ridge-maintained Luis moving westward despite the relatively high latitude that the storm had moving it towards the Northeast Caribbean.

Luis continued to intensify and reached its peak of intensity of sustained 140 mph, 120 kts, winds which maintained for nearly three days with slight fluctuations until reaching the island or Barbuda the morning of September 5th with estimated sustained winds of 135 mph, 115 kts.

Luis was a large storm with an eye of an average 30 to 40 nm wide and an eyewall of nearly the same width. By this time the ridge to the north of the storm had weakened and Luis was turning northwestward while the eyewall directly affected Antigua, St. Barthelemy, St. Martin, and Anguilla.

Also, hurricane conditions were experienced in St. Kitts and Nevis, St. Eustatius, Guadeloupe, and the British Virgin Islands. Hurricane Luis passed around 110 nm northeast of Puerto Rico the morning of September 6th, still the outer bands of the large storm affected the area causing tropical storm conditions through most of the islands, also the US Virgin Islands experienced tropical storm force winds.

The biggest effect of hurricane Luis in Puerto Rico was the chaos that put in test the capability of the government and the people for preparing for a major hurricane. Luis was the first big threat of a major storm in Puerto Rico since hurricane Hugo in 1989 and was a preamble for what the island experienced three years later with hurricane Georges.

Otherwise, heavy surf caused erosion in the north coast and some trees down and moderate river flooding where the results of the passage of the storm through the region.

In the Northern Leeward Islands the story was a lot different with 16 people killed and 2.5 billion dollars in damage making Luis the worst storm to hit the Northeast Caribbean since Hugo in 1989 and David in 1979.

## September 15th-16 1995 Hurricane Marilyn

The extremely active 1995 Hurricane Season proved to be very hazardous for the Northeast Caribbean. Just two weeks after category 4 hurricane Luis, another hurricane was threatening the region.

Marilyn developed from a tropical wave midway between Barbados and the Cape Verde Islands becoming TD #15 the afternoon of September 12th. The depression moved straight towards the Caribbean as it was intensifying and became tropical storm Marilyn six hours after the first advisory was issued. Barely four hours after that, Marilyn became a hurricane.

Marilyn started turning and passed around 45 nm north of Barbados, just north of Martinique, over Dominica and just southwest of Guadeloupe as a category one hurricane during September 14th.

After that, Marilyn continued to strengthen moving northwest and passed over St. Croix the afternoon of the 15th, then between St. Thomas and Culebra, Puerto Rico that night.

Marilyn was a small and intensifying hurricane, and the intensity was estimated to be of sustained 110 mph winds when CPA happened to both islands.

The east and northeast eyewall of the storm passed over St. Thomas bringing disastrous results and the west and northwest eyewall hit Culebra causing heavy damage there. Marilyn remained offshore from Puerto Rico causing tropical storm conditions for the east half and hurricane conditions in the island of Vieques.

Culebra, as mentioned above, experienced the eyewall of the storm. St. Thomas reported a sustained two-minute wind of 105 mph with peak gust to 129 mph, the minimal pressure reported was of 956 millibars while sustained 70 mph winds were still reported, pressure in the center of the eye was estimated to be around 952 millibars.

An unofficial gust of 125 mph was reported in Culebra, Puerto Rico, in the main island the highest wind report was of sustained 41 mph with a gust of 60 mph in Roosevelt Roads, a pressure of 996.5 millibars was measured. San Juan Intl. Airport, TJSJ, reported a peak gust of 45 mph in the early morning of the 16th.

The damage in the main island of Puerto Rico was minimal again but Vieques and Culebra did not escape the core of the hurricane.

Damage in Vieques was moderate with some houses that lost their roofs, power lines down and lots of tree damage.

Culebra had much severe damage as the eyewall blasted through there with many of the homes affected there, trees and power and water services severely damage and with damage estimates comparatively close to those of hurricane Hugo there in 1989.

Marilyn was the worst hurricane to affect Puerto Rican land since hurricane Hugo in 1989.

## July 8, 1996 Hurricane Bertha

Hurricane Bertha was an unusually early call for the people in Puerto Rico and the rest of the region as it passed just northeast of the island during the afternoon of July 8th.

Bertha developed from a tropical wave that emerged off the west coast of Africa and the first advisory on TD #2 was issued the night of the 4th. Bertha was named during the 5th as it moved generally west northwestward towards the Caribbean.

Bertha became a hurricane just before quickly passing through the Northern Leeward Islands and the Virgin Islands during the 8th emerging just north of Puerto Rico late in that day.

The intensity of the storm was 80 to 90 mph sustained and the pressure dropping steadily in the 980s millibars. Bertha passed only 30 nm northeast of Puerto Rico, but tropical storm conditions were felt in the island, hurricane conditions might have been possible in Culebra which was near the southern eyewall of the storm along with St. Thomas.

The highest wind report in Puerto Rico was of 47 mph with a gust to 62 mph in San Juan and a pressure of 992 millibars was measured in Roosevelt Roads.

Damage in the island was relatively minimal with trees down, power outages and river flooding. Three deaths were reported, two died in an automobile accident during the storm and one surfer was drowned.

After affecting the area Bertha moved just north of the Bahamas as a category 2-3 hurricane and made landfall east of Wilmington, NC as a category two hurricane the afternoon of the 12th.

## September 9, 1996 Hurricane Hortense

Hortense was a category one hurricane that caused devastating flooding in Puerto Rico while slowly moving resulting in 18 deaths and nearly 12,000 damage homes, mainly due to flooding.

Hortense developed from a tropical wave east of the Lesser Antilles moving westward, first advisory was issued the morning of September 3rd.

While moving westward, the depression became tropical storm Hortense just before passing near Guadeloupe during the early morning of the 7th. Sustained winds of 53 mph with a gust of 80 mph were reported there.

For the next two days, the storm encountered strong upper-level winds than inhibited any strengthening. Hortense was moving westward but the steering flow became very erratic, and the storm stalled around 100 nm southeast of Puerto Rico.

Then, the storm started to move again but towards the northwest directly towards the southwest coast of the island while strengthening to hurricane intensity the afternoon of the 9th.

Hortense made landfall near Guánica, Puerto Rico at around 2 am AST of September 10th with sustained winds of 80 mph crossing the southwest part of the island for two hours and emerging in the Mona Passage in the vicinity of Cabo Rojo.

This area experience sustained hurricane conditions along with the high elevations of the Central Mountain Range, the rest of the island experienced tropical storm conditions with hurricane conditions in gusts in many areas and extremely heavy rainfall.

The highest wind report in Puerto Rico was an unofficial gust of 110 mph in Guánica but this report is not considered as reliable, otherwise the highest wind report was of 49 mph with a gust of 64 mph in San Juan, Intl. Airport.

A gust of 75 mph was reported in Cuney in the south of San Juan. The main effect from this storm was the heavy rainfall, averages of 15 to 20 inches of rain were reported across the interior of the island with the highest rainfall amount in San Lorenzo, Eastern Interior, with 24.6 inches of rainstorm total.

Hortense became the worst hurricane to hit Puerto Rico since hurricane Hugo in 1989 and the devastating flooding caused 18 casualties, 3 people missing and nearly 12,000 homes affected.

The road system was also hard hit with many bridges left unusable and mudslides covering many roads in the mountainous areas. The main devastation with flooding was experienced in Guayama were the Guamaní River killed several people.

A great deal of the island was declared disaster area and recuperation from the storm took several months for parts of the island.

After causing devastation in Puerto Rico, Hortense passed near Punta Cana, Dominican Republic with winds of 90 mph affecting also the Turks and Caicos Islands with hurricane force winds, later the storm became a powerful category 4, 140 mph, hurricane in the Atlantic while recurving to the north and making landfall in Nova Scotia were sustained hurricane force winds of 76 mph were reported in St. Paul Island.

## September 21st-22, 1998 Hurricane Georges

Hurricane Georges was the worst hurricane to hit Puerto Rico since hurricane "San Ciprian" in 1932. It was a category 3 intensity hurricane that crossed the entire island from east to west leaving destruction and damage across.

Georges developed from a strong tropical wave that emerged from the west coast of Africa in the vicinity of the well-known Cape Verde Islands which in September are a very common place for the development of strong tropical cyclones.

A tropical depression was born in the morning of September 15th and 24 hours later it became tropical storm Georges, moving west in the far eastern Atlantic posing no immediate threat to any land areas.

The following day, Georges steadily intensified becoming a hurricane. By September 19th Georges started a rapid-deepening process which led the storm to reach its peak of intensity in the morning of September 20th with max. Sustained winds of 155mph/135kts and a minimum barometric pressure of 937mb, that happened when the storm was less than 300nm east of the Northern Leeward Islands.

After this point, the storm started a marked weakening trend with the pressure rising 26mb in less than 12 hours and the eye becoming less distinct. This weakening could be related to northerly upper-level wind shear that disrupted the structure of the hurricane due to an upper-level anticyclone located over the eastern Caribbean.

Then early in the morning of September 21st, Georges made landfall in Antigua with top sustained winds of 115mph/100kts passing hours later over St. Kitts and Nevis still with the same intensity.

With the intensity decreasing to 110mph/95kts shortly after passing St. Kitts and Nevis, Georges found better upper-level conditions with the shear diminishing and the outflow improving as the storm was approaching Puerto Rico.

Later, the eye of the hurricane moved over St. Croix, U. S. Virgin Island and approaching Vieques, Puerto Rico.

Satellite and radar images from Puerto Rico showed Georges becoming better organized as it was getting closer to Vieques. Georges passed over Vieques in the mid afternoon and around 6pm the eye of the hurricane made landfall in Eastern Puerto Rico with max. sustained winds of 115mph/100kts and a pressure of 967mb as the storm was intensifying and was back to category 3 intensity.

This increase in the winds was based on 110mph/96kts sustained winds measured in Fajardo, Puerto Rico when the eyewall of the storm came ashore, this report was the reason for increasing Georges back to category 3 intensity at landfall in Puerto Rico.

In addition to that, the WSR-88D Doppler Radar in San Juan estimated sustained winds of 115mph/100kts when Georges was over Puerto Rico.

Georges continued in a west/west-northwest direction over Eastern Puerto Rico with a very impressive eastern eyewall showed in the San Juan Radar.

Georges passed 20nm south of San Juan at around 8pm, right over my hometown of Gurabo where the calm was experienced for more than 30 minutes followed by very turbulent and strong winds from the south associated with the very strong eastern eyewall of the hurricane which lasted for several hours.

San Juan Intl. Airport measured sustained winds of 79mph/69kts with a gust of 93mph/81kts at around 7:20pm of September 21st.

The main reason for measuring lower winds in San Juan was the blockage of the Mountain Range south of the city, while cities like Caguas in Central Eastern, Puerto Rico where much affected by the strong winds also by the "Fujiwara Effect" of acceleration between mountains and valleys.

The eye of the storm then continued moving now west over Central Puerto Rico and the land interaction for many hours caused the storm to weaken back to category 2 intensity with 110mph/95kts sustained winds as it was crossing the western part of the island.

The eye of hurricane Georges left Western Puerto Rico at around 1am September 22nd still as a strong category 2 intensity hurricane 7 hours after landfall.

Georges continued over the Mona Passage passing over Mona and making landfall in Eastern Dominican Republic with sustained winds of 120mph/105kts and a pressure of 962mb later in the morning of September 22nd.

The storm started to move in a more west-northwest direction over Dominican Republic passing just north of Santo Domingo and into the high mountains of Central Hispaniola.

The storm lasted 21 hours over land weakening to 75mph/65kts in the morning of September 23rd making landfall later that day with the same intensity over Eastern Cuba.

Still with a very impressive upper-level outflow, the storm left the north coast of Cuba by late afternoon September 24th and moving in a more northwesterly direction.

Georges made landfall in Key West, Florida in the morning of September 25th with sustained winds of 105mph/90kts and a pressure of 981mb and then continued to move over the Gulf of Mexico intensifying further to 110mph/95kts and making its final landfall near Biloxi, Mississippi on the morning of September 28th with max. sustained winds of 105mph/90kts and a pressure of 964mb.

Georges moved inland and became quasi-stationary being downgraded to tropical storm and dissipating early in the morning of October 1st.

## The Path of Destruction.......

Georges was the second most destructive hurricane of the 1998 hurricane season after hurricane Mitch. A total of 602 deaths are directly associated to the path of the hurricane.

This happened mainly in the Dominican Republic and Haiti due to the very heavy rains which caused a lot of flooding and mud slides as the storm came through Hispaniola, the Leeward Islands to the USVI, Puerto Rico, Dominican Republic and Haiti, Cuba, the Florida Keys and the states of Mississippi, Louisiana, Alabama, and the Florida Panhandle.

In the United States the damages estimates are of nearly $6 billion dollars. In terms of damage, hurricane Georges left a path of destruction from

Puerto Rico was hit hard by Georges with up to 72,605 houses affected by the storm of which 28,005 houses were destroyed.

More than 26,000 people took shelter during the storm and a very high number was still in shelters during the aftermath of the hurricane.

A 95% of the banana crop was destroyed and 75% of the coffee crop was lost. The entire electric system of the island was shut down by the hurricane and nearly the entire island was also without water. So far only 30,000 customers lost telephone service mainly due to the new fiber optic lines installed all around the island.

The road infrastructure was very affected mainly by flooding and mudslides. The total damage estimates for Puerto Rico are of $1,907,026,374.

## October 21, 1999 Tropical Storm José:

Hurricane José developed from the coast of Africa and the first advisory by NHC was issued the afternoon of October 17th as it was moving west towards the Lesser Antilles. The system was classified as a tropical storm the 18th when it was 400 nm east of the islands.

As the storm was approaching, a more northwesterly track was assumed by the storm as a weakness in the high was northwest of the cyclone.

José became a hurricane late in the 19th while centered about 150 nm east of the Lesser Antilles, the storm kept intensifying and peaked at an intensity of 85 kts, 100 mph, sustained winds while approaching the island of Antigua the morning of the 20th.

The hurricane then started moving in a more west-northwesterly track and moved over Antigua at midday of the 20th with sustained winds of 80 kts, 90 mph, as this happened, strong southwest upper-level winds started to affect the cyclone and made it weaken to tropical storm intensity, the eye of the weakening hurricane passed near St. Barthelemy and St. Martin late in the 20th and over Tortola in the British Virgin Islands early in the 21st, by this time the cyclone had weakened to tropical storm intensity estimated to be near 60 kts, 70 mph.

Tropical Storm José then passed just north of the US Virgin Islands and around 20 nm north of Culebra, Puerto Rico early in the afternoon of the 21st and later that afternoon around 45 nm northeast of Fajardo, Puerto Rico.

The Tropical storm force winds were measured unofficially in Luquillo early in the 21st with around 40-45 mph sustained with a peak gust of 55 mph.

This was the only report of tropical storm intensity winds in the island, the higher elevations high have gotten tropical storm force winds also. Damage in Puerto Rico was light with river flooding and some wind damage in Culebra were power was also lost during a short period.

After affecting the area, José regained hurricane intensity while recurving out in the open Atlantic and losing tropical characteristics.

## November 17, 1999 Hurricane Lenny

Hurricane Lenny was a historic storm for many reasons, especially due to its unusual path from west to east across the Caribbean, so late in the season and the high intensity, 155 mph, that the storm attained during its trek across the Northeast Caribbean.

Lenny developed from a low-pressure area, LPA, in the Western Caribbean and this system organized enough to be classified as a tropical depression during the afternoon of the 13th around 150 nm south of Grand Cayman Island.

The morning of the 14th, Lenny was named as a tropical storm while moving generally to the east during the next few days.

On the 15th, Lenny became a hurricane while south of Jamaica and weakened briefly while passing to the south of Haiti, then the storm continued to intensify as it was forecasted to directly hit Puerto Rico. Lenny was moving generally to the east-northeast and it began to rapidly intensify when south of Puerto Rico as it passed around 75 nm southeast of the island the morning of the 17th as a category 4 hurricane.

Lenny then passed around 15 nm south of St. Croix bringing the northern eyewall over the island.

By this time the storm was at its peak intensity of 135 kts, 155 mph, sustained winds, and a pressure of 933 millibars but these winds were confined to the southeast eyewall which did not affect St. Croix.

As the storm moved away from St. Croix, it encountered very weak steering currents and moved slowly while approaching the St. Martin-Anguilla area.

Despite favorable upper-level winds Lenny weakened as it moved over St. Martin during the 18th with estimated sustained winds of 110 kts, 125 mph, and weakened further as it was nearly stationary in the area becoming a tropical storm just south of St. Barthelemy and moving east-southeast passing over Antigua late in the 19th with winds estimated to be down to 55 kts, 65 mph.

Lenny then continued to move away and dissipated during the day of the 23rd around 600 nm east of the Leeward Islands.

Damage in Puerto Rico was again very minimal with some mud slides, trees down and heavy surf in the southeast coast which brought erosion. Vieques possibly got hurricane conditions and wind damage was more noticeable there.

The highest wind report in Puerto Rico was a gust of 48 mph in Roosevelt Roads, nearly 6 inches of rain were reported throughout the event.

## August 22, 2000 Hurricane Debby

Debby developed from a strong tropical wave that emerged off the coast of Africa and was classified as a tropical depression the afternoon of August 19th, Debby was named later in the 20th and despite vertical shear the storm continued to intensify becoming a hurricane with a peak intensity of 75 kts, 85 mph, early in the 21st.

The strong upper-level winds made the storm weaken slowly but steadily as it moved over the Northern Leeward Islands, the British Virgin Islands and 30 nm northeast of Puerto Rico during the 22nd.

By this time Debby's intensity was estimated to be sustained 65 kts, 75 mph.

Debby continued to move just north of Puerto Rico and weakening while moving just north of Hispaniola as a tropical storm and finally dissipating in the Windward Passage in the 24th due to strong vertical wind shear.

Even though the storm moved very close to Puerto Rico, the weak quadrant of the storm was the one that affected the island and no reports of tropical storm force winds were measured, the main effect of Debby in the area was very heavy rainfall that caused flooding in the entire country, especially in the area of Ponce and the northern coastal valleys, this heavy rainfall came after the storm moved away from the area when the main feeder band brought up to 12.63 inches of rain measured at Rio Piedras.

An indirect death was also reported when a man fell of the roof of his house trying to remove and antenna.

## September 15, 2004 Tropical Storm Jeanne

Tropical Storm Jeanne developed from a rather weak tropical wave that crossed the Atlantic Ocean and organized quite rapidly just east of the Leeward Islands.

The first advisory was issued by the National Hurricane Center during the day of the 13th and a tropical storm had formed in the 14th as the system was slowly moving over the Leeward Islands.

Jeanne found favorable upper-level winds and continued to strengthen becoming nearly a hurricane when landfall occurred at around midday AST in the 15th near Maunabo, Puerto Rico with an official intensity estimate of 60 kts, 70 mph, sustained winds.

For the next 6 to 8 hours the center of the storm crossed Puerto Rico exiting the island near Arecibo but finally emerging out in the ocean near Aguadilla in the night of the 15th.

Jeanne was the worst tropical cyclone to hit Puerto Rico since hurricane Georges in 1998. Wind damage specially in the eastern side of the island was moderate with many trees down, power lines and poles, signs blown out and some roofs of houses and businesses that were damaged.

Flooding was also experienced throughout the island and storm surge flooding was reported in Humacao and Yabucoa. The entire island at one point was left without power but this was mainly due to a mistake made by operators of the electric system, even with that, the areas affected worst by the wind were nearly one week without power as it was the case in places like southern Caguas.

The highest wind report was an unofficial report of 63 mph sustained winds in Salinas with a peak gust of 71 mph. San Juan reported sustained winds of 49 mph with a peak gust of 71 mph.

Hurricane conditions may have been experienced in the area north of the center of the storm, specially from Yabucoa northward to Naguabo and the high elevations.

The highest rainfall amount reported was in Vieques with 23.75 inches of rainstorm total.

This storm proved to be a hazard to the government and people due to its rapid intensification just prior to affecting the area with preparations completed the same morning that the cyclone hit the island.

After hitting Puerto Rico, Jeanne officially became a hurricane and made landfall near Punta Cana, Dominican Republic with winds of 70 kts, 80 mph.

Then, the hurricane weakened over land causing catastrophic flooding specially in Haiti were over 2,900 people died especially in Gonaives.

Jeanne emerged as a tropical depression and moved northward over the Atlantic and was influenced again by a strong mid-surface ridge that made it turn in a loop back towards the west as it deepened back to hurricane intensity making landfall in Abaco Island, Bahamas early in the 25th with winds of 100 kts, 115 MP.

Later, on that day and early in the 26th over Stuart, Florida with winds of 105 kts, 120 mph, did plenty of damage in both the Bahamas and Florida.

It was horrible because hurricane Frances hit the same area just two weeks earlier.

Every year, between June and November, Puerto Rico is threatened by storms or hurricanes due to its geographical location.

Historically, the island has been hit by several hurricanes of category three or more, which have left in its wake multiple damages and thousands of people homeless.

Although 19 years ago that Puerto Rico does not feel the scourge of a hurricane's strong category, after Georges in 1998.

Several storms have affected the region leaving a feeling of fury or nature rage. In fact, weather experts warn that after many years the impact of a cyclone.

The island must be prepared for a similar or higher rank. Although 15 years ago that Puerto Rico does not feel the scourge of a hurricane's strong category, after Georges in 1998.

Facing hurricane seasons in this island, warnings will always be active.

# CHAPTER 5

## The tropical storms from 1851 to 2012.

A whiteboard at a FEMA tactical relief operation center in Louisiana notes the number of named storms. It shows the hurricanes and counts down of the remaining months or days in 2008 during the Atlantic hurricane season.

### Hurricane from 1980 through 2014

The Atlantic hurricane season is the period in a year when hurricanes usually form in the Atlantic Ocean. Tropical cyclones in the North Atlantic are called hurricanes, tropical storms, or tropical depressions.

In addition, there have been several storms over the years that have not been fully tropical and are categorized as subtropical depressions and subtropical storms.

Even though subtropical storms and subtropical depressions are not technically as strong as tropical cyclones, the damages can still be devastating.

Worldwide, tropical cyclone activity peaks in late summer when the difference between temperatures aloft and sea surface temperatures is the greatest. However, each basin has its own seasonal patterns. On a worldwide scale, May is the least active month, while September is the most active.

In the Northern Atlantic Ocean, a distinct hurricane season occurs from June 1 to November 30, sharply peaking from late August through

September; the season's climatological peak of activity occurs around September 10 each season.

This is the norm, but in 1938, the Atlantic hurricane season started as early as January 3.

Tropical disturbances that reach tropical storm intensity are named from a pre-determined list.

On an average, 10.1 named storms occur each season, with an average of 5.9 becoming hurricanes and 2.5 becoming major hurricanes category 3 or greater.

The most active season was 2005, during which 28 tropical cyclones formed, of which a record 15 became hurricanes. The least active season was 1914, with only one known tropical cyclone developing during that year.

The Atlantic hurricane season is a time when most tropical cyclones are expected to develop across the northern Atlantic Ocean. It is currently defined as the time frame from June 1 through November 30, though in the past the season was defined as a shorter time frame. During the season, regular tropical weather outlooks are issued by the National Hurricane Center, and coordination between the Weather Prediction Center and National Hurricane Center occurs for systems which have not formed yet but could develop during the next three to seven days.

The basic concept of a hurricane season began during 1935, when dedicated wire circuits known as hurricane circuits began to be set up along the Gulf and Atlantic coasts. This process was completed by 1955.

It was originally the time frame when the tropics were monitored routinely for tropical cyclone activity and was originally defined as from June 15 through October 31.

Over the years, the beginning date was shifted back to June 1, while the end date was shifted to November 1 before settling on November 30, 1965. This was when hurricane reconnaissance planes were sent out to fly across the Atlantic and Gulf of Mexico on a routine basis to look for potential tropical cyclones, in the years before the continuous weather satellite era.

Since regular satellite surveillance began, hurricane hunter aircraft fly only into storm areas which are first spotted by satellite imagery.

During the hurricane season, the National Hurricane Center routinely issues their Tropical Weather Outlook product, which identifies areas of concern within the tropics which could develop into tropical cyclones.

If systems occur outside the defined hurricane season, special Tropical Weather Outlooks will be issued. Routine coordination occurs at 1700 UTC each day between the Weather Prediction Center and National Hurricane Center to identify systems for the pressure maps three to seven days into the future within the tropics, and points for existing tropical cyclones six to seven days into the future.

Possible tropical cyclones are depicted with a closed isobar, while systems with less certainty to develop are depicted as "spot lows" with no isobar surrounding them.

The North Atlantic hurricane database, or HURDAT, is the database for all tropical storms and hurricanes for the Atlantic Ocean, Gulf of Mexico, and Caribbean Sea, including those that have made landfall in the United States.

The original database of six-hourly positions and intensities were put together in the 1960s in support of the Apollo space program to help provide statistical track forecast guidance. In the intervening years, this database which is now freely and easily accessible on the Internet from the National Hurricane Center's, NHC, webpage.

It has been utilized for a wide variety of uses climatic change studies, seasonal forecasting, risk assessment for county emergency managers, analysis of potential losses for insurance and business interests, intensity forecasting techniques and verification of official and various model predictions of track and intensity.

HURDAT was not designed with all of these uses in mind when it was first put together and not all of them may be appropriate given its original motivation.

HURDAT contains numerous systematic as well as some random errors in the database. Additionally, analysis techniques have changed over the years at NHC as their understanding of tropical cyclones has developed, leading to biases in the historical database.

Another difficulty in applying the hurricane database to studies concerned with land falling events is the lack of exact location, time, and intensity at hurricane landfall.

HURDAT is regularly updated annually to reflect the previous season's activity. The older portion of the database has been regularly revised since 2001.

The first time, in 2001, led to the addition of tropical cyclone tracks for the years 1851 to 1885.

The second time was August 2002 when Hurricane Andrew was upgraded to a Category 5. Recent efforts into uncovering undocumented historical hurricanes in the late 19th and 20th centuries by various researchers have greatly increased our knowledge of these past events.

Possible changes for the years 1951 onward are not yet incorporated into the HURDAT database. Because of all these issues, a re-analysis of the Atlantic hurricane database is being attempted that will be completed in three years.

In addition to the groundbreaking work by Partagas, additional analyses, digitization and quality control of the data was carried out by researchers at the NOAA Hurricane Research Division funded by the NOAA Office of Global Programs.

This re-analysis will continue to progress through the remainder of the 20th century.

The National Hurricane Center's Best Track Change Committee has approved changes for a few recent cyclones, such as Hurricane Andrew. Official changes to the Atlantic hurricane database are approved by the National Hurricane Center Best Track Change Committee.

Thus, research conducted by Chris Land Sea and colleagues as part of the Atlantic hurricane database reanalysis project are submitted through this review process. Not all Land Sea's recommendations are accepted by the Committee.

# CHAPTER 6

## Dealing with Disasters

Every year disasters take lives, cause significant damage, inhibit development, and contribute to conflict and forced migration. Unfortunately, the trend is an upward one.

In May 2017, policymakers, and disaster management experts from over 180 countries gathered in Cancun, Mexico, to discuss ways to counter this trend.

In the middle of the Cancun summit, news arrived that large parts of Sri Lanka were devastated by floods and landslides, killing at least 150 and displacing almost half a million people.

It was a harsh reminder of the summit participants' challenging task of covering the way towards reducing disaster losses "significantly" by the year 2030 based on the Sendai Framework for Disaster Risk Reduction.

Adopted in 2015, the Sendai Framework outlines seven targets and four priorities for action to prevent new, and reduce existing, disaster risks to economic, physical, social, cultural, health or environmental assets and lives of persons, businesses, communities, and countries.

Since then, in China, a village in the Sichuan province has been devastated by a landslide and rescuers are still looking for missing people.

Disasters occur when people are affected by natural or technical hazards. This happens when lives are lost, or property is destroyed.

As the Swiss writer Max Frisch observed in his 1979 book 'Man in the Holocene', "-only human beings can recognize catastrophes, provided they survive them; nature recognizes no catastrophes."

Research conducted in Sri Lanka suggests that while heavy rainfall was the trigger for the flooding, the root causes of the disaster were social, widespread poverty, conflict-induced migration, and problematic land-use practices. These characteristics are not homogeneous, meaning different places and people are affected differently.

The social characteristics of communities are extremely important for hazard managers because they increase peoples' vulnerability to hazards.

A global community that is dedicated to reducing disaster losses over the next decade must address these social root causes of disaster. If not, the lofty goals of the Sendai Framework will remain mysterious.

Understandably, socially disadvantaged communities exposed to hazards have to date received the most attention from DRR specialists. This is because hazards tend to harm predominantly those social groups that were already disadvantaged before a disaster.

Large focus has been placed on "underdeveloped" or "developing" nations, where the social disadvantage factors are particularly obvious. For example, while studying the social aspects of food insecurity during droughts in the Sahel region in the mid-1980s, scientists showed that low-wealth families with many children were particularly susceptible to chronic food insecurity.

You must keep in mind that groups of people living in places where the overall socio-economic status is higher can also be vulnerable to hazards, and little is known about these groups.

The assumption that all members of affluent societies are somehow immune to disasters seems to be broadly shared, perhaps because vulnerability may be less obvious. This misbelief seems to be reinforced by various attempts to index and compare the vulnerability of communities, regions, or whole nations.

In fact, making inferences about disaster vulnerability based on aggregated economic characteristics often leads to misleading conclusions. This problem is known as the 'ecological fallacy', where relationships on the aggregate level do not necessarily hold on the individual level.

For instance, research from the 1990s demonstrated that homeless people in Tokyo, at the time one of the wealthiest cities in the world, were far more vulnerable to earthquake hazards than the average resident.

Problematically, emergency planning by government overlooked this 'invisible' sub-population. In this case, the 'ecological fallacy' meant there was a tendency for emergency planning activities to be directed toward a higher socio-economic class.

Additionally, research conducted in the wake of Hurricane Katrina's impact on New Orleans in 2005 has shown that socio-economically disadvantaged households and communities were disproportionally affected by the hurricane. These people lacked the capabilities to prepare for, respond to and recover from the event.

These examples, from affluent and less affluent countries, suggest the need to consider social vulnerability in more geographically and demographically nuanced ways when implementing DRR activities.

On the one hand, poorer communities might bring alternative capabilities to DRR that are non-financial.

On the other hand, ignoring existing social disadvantage within affluent contexts risks significant loss of life and property, and forgoes the opportunity to improve the circumstances of the affected sub-populations.

Across most Caribbean islands, hazard exposure is about the same, but research shows that poverty and social inequality drastically magnify the severity of disasters.

Haiti, where eight out of every 10 people live on less than $4 a day, offers an example of how capitalism, gender and history converge to compound storm damage.

The country is among the Western Hemisphere's poorest in large part because of imperialism.

After Haitians successfully overthrew their European enslavers in 1804, global powers economically stifled the island. From 1915 to 1934, the U.S. first militarily occupied Haiti, and then followed a policy of intervention that continues to have lasting effects on its governance.

International interference and the resulting weak institutions, in turn, impeded development, poverty reduction and empowerment efforts.

In such a context, disasters aggravate a country's numerous existing social vulnerabilities. Take gender, for example. Mental health professionals offering support to victims after Haiti's 2010 earthquake found that an extraordinarily high number of displaced women. Up to

75 percent had experienced sexual violence. This prior trauma worsened the women's post-disaster stress responses.

Inequality and underdevelopment are perhaps less marked in the rest of the Caribbean, but from Antigua and Barbuda to St. Kitts and Nevis, socioeconomic problems are now complicating both disaster preparedness and response.

Across the region, people spend most of their income on daily essentials like food, clean water, shelter, and medicine, with little left over for greeting Irma and Maria with lifesaving hurricane-resilient roofs, storm shutters, solar generators and first aid kits.

For the poor, emergency radios and satellite telephones that could warn of impending disasters are largely unaffordable, as is homeowners' insurance to hasten recovery.

Poorer Caribbean residents also tend to live in the most disaster-prone areas because housing is cheaper on unstable deforested hillsides and eroding riverbanks.

This exponentially increases the danger they face. The low construction quality of these dwellings offers less protection during storms while, post-disaster, emergency vehicles may not be able to access these areas.

Caribbean women will also continue to be at particular risk well after Maria passes. In a region where gender roles remain quite rigid, women are typically tasked with childcare, harvesting, cooking, cleaning, washing and the like.

Even in post-disaster settings, women are expected to perform household labor. So, when water supplies are contaminated, with sewage, E. coli, salmonella, cholera, yellow fever, and hepatitis A, among others, women are disproportionately exposed to illness.

The work of nourishing the spirits and bodies of others when food and water shortages occur is also thrust onto women, even though they generally have less access to income and credit than men.

# CHAPTER 7

## Hurricane Maria

It all began on September 20, 2017, at about 6:15 am....

The morning after Hurricane Maria destroyed Puerto Rico, I tried calling my relatives in the United States. It was impossible. All communications were destroyed.

I decided to send my sister a letter. That was on September 21. I heard from her on Oct. 15. She was happy to hear that my dad and I were fine. I assured her that we were ok, but that Puerto Rico was destroyed.

We lost contact once again....

Nearly a month after the hurricane, Puerto Rico was still struggling with a near-total information blackout. Some 85 percent of the island lacked electricity, and several remote mountain communities have yet to be visited by relief workers.

The death toll rose rapidly because of the as lack of fuel, food shortages and infectious illnesses took their toll. Over 100 people were missing.

The island was crippled in part, I thank the federal government's underwhelming early hurricane response. The historic storm played its role, of course, destroying homes, triggering mudslides, and rendering roadways blocked.

The Trump administration delayed dispatching military personnel and material relief until after the hurricane made landfall, and let the Jones Act waiver lapse, reducing the number of ships that can bring aid to the island. These actions have slowed recovery considerably.

NATURE'S RAGE IN THE CARIBBEAN

Numerous commentators, including Ret. Lt. Gen. Russel Honoré, who ran the U.S. military's 2005 Hurricane Katrina relief operation, criticized the Trump administration's Puerto Rico storm response.

Others have contrasted it with the all-hands-on-deck support seen by Harvey and Irma victims in Texas and Florida.

Based on my experience researching equity and inclusion in U.S. policy, racial bias may explain these disparate relief efforts, at least in part.

Environmental disasters lay bare existing inequalities like prejudice and poverty. So, in a place like Puerto Rico, where nearly 99 percent of the population is Latino, discriminatory decision-making can hurt the community's capacity to recover.

In Texas and Florida, the president responded swiftly, visiting these southern states in a matter of days. In Puerto Rico, on the other hand, President Trump arrived to survey the wreckage two weeks after Maria struck.

President Trump vowed to stand with Texas and Florida "every single day" to help them "restore, recover and rebuild," he seemed to mock Puerto Ricans' dilemma at an Oct. 6 Hispanic Heritage Month event.

Trump even threatened to withdraw federal aid from Puerto Rico altogether, even though some communities have yet to see a penny.

There is practical evidence that skin color impacts federal assistance. A 2007 study performed by researchers at Stanford and UCLA found that Americans are less willing to support extensive taxpayer-funded disaster relief when the victim population is not white.

Signs of racial bias in the current federal relief efforts go beyond Puerto Rico. The U.S. Virgin Islands, where 98 percent of the population identifies as black or of African ancestry, were also battered by both Hurricanes Irma and Maria, leaving residents "in survival mode." The Trump administration has also largely ignored their suffering.

There are likely other explanations for why America's Caribbean citizens are seeing such dissimilar post-storm treatment.

One is political influence. These two U.S. territories were certainly facing an uphill disaster recovery process because unlike, Texas and Florida, Puerto Rico and the U.S. Virgin Islands don't have representatives defending their interests in Congress.

Allegiance is another likely factor. Facing historic disapproval ratings, President Trump's agenda has also narrowed toward rallying his base.

It's predictable, then, that the president worked diligently to help Texas and Florida. Those states supported him in 2016. He neglected Caribbean residents, who could not vote in a presidential election.

I would argue that the differential post-hurricane treatment exceeded these political disadvantages and reflects racial bias.

Throughout the disaster relief effort, President Trump's vocabulary has highlighted just how different Puerto Rico and the U.S. Virgin Islands are from mainland America. He has called the islands' leadership "poor" and "opportunistic" and blamed Puerto Ricans for the financial crisis that's now confounding the island's recovery.

Trump also complained on Puerto Ricans for "wanting everything to be done for them" and failing to contribute more to the relief efforts.

According to Trump, not aid workers but Puerto Ricans themselves should be out distributing food and water.

I have spent some time studying urban policy toward communities of color, so coded language like this raises red flags.

It is especially concerning given President Trump's own problematic history dealing with race.

On the campaign trail, Trump antagonized the Black Lives Matter movement, and as president he defended the violence of white supremacists in Charlottesville.

Recent U.S. history also offers examples suggesting that communities of color are neglected when disaster hits.

Look at New Orleans after Hurricane Katrina. This is the classic case study. After the city's evacuation plan failed, black Americans were left stranded and desperate for up to 14 days while the federal government's belated and dysfunctional rescue operation struck.

Assessing the situation, rapper Kanye West famously went off script at a live fundraiser for hurricane victims, declaring, "George Bush doesn't care about black people."

In April 2014, residents of Flint, Michigan, a predominantly black community, began falling ill after the highly contaminated Flint River became their only water source. Community members raised concern about the foul-smelling water coming out of their faucets, and doctors alerted state and federal officials about elevated lead levels in the water.

Even so, state officials did not acknowledge Flint's crisis until September 2015, after 91 residents had been diagnosed with waterborne bacterial illnesses. And only this year did the city finally agree to replace their water lines. The city clean water in 2020.

In short, though environmental disasters don't see race, people do and if bias influences the decision-making of those in power, survivors will feel it.

Puerto Rico's demographics diverge from that of the U.S. general population, where just 18 percent of people identify as Latino and 13 percent as black. President Trump's behavior seems to reflect that racial difference, whether he knows it or not.

Hurricane Maria flooded Puerto Rico with 20 inches of rain and damaged it with 150 mph winds for over 30 hours.

This catastrophe resulted a humanitarian crisis. It has been widely reported worldwide that 80 percent of the island was without electricity or not enough drinking water.

Communication was another story. The radio, television, telephones, and internet took a long time to recover.

What outsiders were unable to see, maybe, is that an entire culture has arisen around the catastrophe caused by Hurricane Maria.

One with typically catastrophic traits was that there was a shortage of materials to build or repair homes. There are still emotional traumas, economic catastrophe, and environmental devastation.

Puerto Ricans are currently facing a dramatically different way of life, which means our relatives and friends too.

Nothing about life look like anything close to normal. An estimated 100,000 homes and buildings were destroyed in the storm.

Over 90 percent of the island's transportation was damaged or destroyed. Not only are there shortages of water and electricity, but also food, highways, bridges, security forces and medical facilities.

It was unsafe to go outside at night. An island-wide curfew was lifted. There were no streetlights, stoplights, or police, driving or walking around. It was very dangerous after dark.

The official total of missing people fluctuated for a long time. Considering Puerto Rico's hazardous conditions and limited health care services, the numbers will be reported in a future date.

Everyone was aware about the epidemic diseases, including leptospirosis and cholera. Health concerns were further stoked by the delays and disarray of the various federal agencies. They took months in handling real emergencies.

There is a deep uncertainty over every Puerto Rican's future. There is post-traumatic stress involved in surviving in an overwhelming situation like this.

Hurricane Maria has changed the modern history of Puerto Rico. For those who are curious about storms and hurricane in our enchanted island, keep ready this book and your will know what we go through every hurricane season.

To understand why I am so angry at this time about the federal government, I will tell you more about myself...

I was born in Ponce, Puerto Rico but grew up in the states. My father was in the army; therefore, we were relocated many times,

I took it upon myself to learn Spanish. I speak fluent Spanish and I consider myself fully bilingual. To me, Hispanics are represented by nearly all racial and ethnic groups. There are white Hispanics, black Hispanics, Asian Hispanics, Arab Hispanics, indigenous Hispanics, etc. Having said that, Trump is obviously a bigot and this stereotype fits into his narrow worldview. However, the other factor, which I believe is equally important is Puerto Rico's vague political status as a "Commonwealth".

With no electoral votes and no electoral power, it's easy to understand why Puerto Rico has received short shrift. It was a state, as has been proposed many times, this would not have happened.

I have the same opinion that Trump's inherent racism plays a significant part in the slow federal aid and Puerto Rico's struggles to recover.

Politics has played a part in emergency planning and recovery for several years. Our federal government should do more to assist PR and the US Virgin Islands. However, how much of their struggle to recover is also due to the landscape, geography, and lack of a robust infrastructure?

MY first reaction to Trump's visit to our island was "DUH." Trump's despicable and racist comments to and about the Puerto Rico should in and of themselves be grounds for saying he is unfit to be the President of the United States. United States treatment of Puerto Ricans, who are CITIZENS, is a national disgrace.

I Just want to point out that the percent of U.S. Virgin Islanders identifying as solely or partially black or African American is 78%, not 98%.

As I'm sure you're aware, Black, and multi-racial identity in the United States and Caribbean is tense and complicated landscape because of the stigma and social stratification historically attached to that identity.

Where sources wander on this population, for many of the above outlined reasons, and I too came across sources that projected the Black/African Ancestry population of the USVI to be in mid to high 70's, I chose more recent census projections that I felt were most reflective of the realities throughout the Caribbean.

Hurricane Maria is regarded as the worst natural disaster on record in Dominica and caused catastrophic damage and a major humanitarian crisis in Puerto Rico.

The tenth-most intense Atlantic hurricane on record, Maria was the thirteenth named storm, seventh consecutive hurricane, fourth major hurricane, and the second Category 5 hurricane of the hyperactive 2017 Atlantic hurricane season.

At its peak, the hurricane caused catastrophic damage and numerous fatalities across the northeastern Caribbean, compounding recovery efforts in the areas of the Leeward Islands already struck by Hurricane Irma just two weeks prior. Maria was the third consecutive major hurricane to threaten the Leeward Islands in two weeks, after Irma made landfall in several of the islands two weeks prior and Hurricane Jose passed dangerously close bringing tropical storm force winds to Barbuda.

Originating from a tropical wave, Maria became a tropical storm on September 16, east of the Lesser Antilles. Remarkably favorable environmental conditions allowed the storm to undergo explosive intensification as it approached the island arc.

The hurricane reached Category 5 strength on September 18 upon making landfall in Dominica, producing extreme winds across the entire island.

Afterwards, Maria achieved its peak intensity over the eastern Caribbean with maximum sustained winds of 175 mph, 280 km/h, and a pressure of 908 mbar, hPa: 26.81 inHg, making it the tenth-most intense Atlantic hurricane on record.

Weakening slightly, but retaining its ferocious winds, Maria struck land weakened the hurricane, though it regained some strength as it moved northeast of The Bahamas.

Moving slowly to the north, Maria gradually degraded and weakened to a tropical storm on September 28. Embedded in the westerly's, Maria accelerated toward the east and later east-northeast over the open Atlantic, becoming extra tropical on September 30,     2017 and dissipating by October 3, 2017.

As of October 10, 2017, at least 94 people are confirmed to have been killed by the hurricane: 51 in Puerto Rico, 28 in Dominica, 5 in the Dominican Republic, 4 in the contiguous United States, 3 in Haiti, 2 in Guadeloupe, and 1 in the United States Virgin Islands.

Hundreds of others, mostly in Dominica and Puerto Rico, are still missing. Maria created catastrophic damage to the entirety of Dominica, which suffered an island-wide communication blackout.

A great deal of the housing stock and infrastructure were left beyond repair, while the island's lush vegetation had been practically eradicated. The islands of Guadeloupe and Martinique endured widespread flooding, damaged roofs, and uprooted trees.

Puerto Rico suffered catastrophic damage, including destruction of its previously damaged electrical grid. For weeks in Maria's wake, most of the island's population suffered from flooding and lack of resources, compounded by the slow relief process.

The total losses from the hurricane are estimated at between $15.9 and $95 billion, 2017 USD, mostly in Puerto Rico, making Maria's cost comparable to that of previous Hurricanes Irma and Harvey.

The National Hurricane Center began monitoring two tropical waves on September 13. The easternmost wave quickly spun up into what would become Hurricane Lee, while the western one continued moving generally westward. With generally favorable conditions in the disturbance's path, development into a tropical cyclone seemed likely.

During those two days the disturbance became better organized by September 16, convective banding became established around a poorly organized circulation.

As the system was an imminent threat to land despite the center not being well-defined, the NHC initiated advisories on it as "Potential Tropical Cyclone Fifteen" at 15:00 UTC, in accordance with a policy change enacted at the start of the season.

A mid-level ridge anchored north of the disturbance steered it generally west-northwest into a region highly favorable for further development. Sea surface temperatures of 84 °F, 29 °C, low wind shear, and ample moisture were anticipated to foster strengthening to hurricane-status before the system reached the Lesser Antilles'.

As the disturbance continued to grow increasingly well-defined throughout the day, it was later upgraded to a moderate-range tropical storm—based on satellite estimates—at 21:00 UTC that day, receiving the name Maria.

At that time, Maria was situated 620 mi, 1,000 km, east-southeast of the Lesser Antilles.

A central dense overcast and favorable outflow developed atop the center of circulation, which enabled Maria to become further organized throughout the early morning hours of September 17, 2017.

After a brief intrusion of dry air exposed the circulation, a convective burst occurred over the center and intensification resumed. Hurricane Hunters investigating the system observed surface winds of 74 mph, 119 km/h, and a formative eye feature.

Accordingly, the NHC upgraded Maria to hurricane status at 21:00 UTC. Expansion of the central dense overcast and an increasingly complete eye wall signaled steady intensification throughout the overnight of September 17–18, 2017.

Considerable lightning activity was identified within the hurricane's core early on September 18 and statistical models indicated a high probability of rapid intensification.

Explosive strengthening took place shortly thereafter, with aircraft reconnaissance finding surface winds of 120 mph, 195 km/h, and a central pressure of 959 mbar, hPa: 28.32 inHg, making Maria a Category 3 hurricane on the Saffir–Simpson scale, and hence a major hurricane.

Additionally, radar data revealed a well-defined 12 mi, 19 km, wide eye. The eye contracted slightly to 9 mi, 14 km, as intensification continued, and the system reached Category 4 strength by 21:00 UTC.

Radar imagery of Hurricane Maria from Puerto Rico at 09:36 UTC, 5:36 a.m. local time, shortly before it stopped transmitting data.

Rapid intensification culminated late on September 18, with Maria achieving Category 5 status just 15 mi, 25 km, east-southeast of Dominica.

Hurricane Hunters observed surface winds of 160 mph (260 km/h) and a pressure of 925 mbar, hPa; 27.32 inHg, at this time. Maria made landfall in Dominica at 01:15 UTC on September 19, becoming the first Category 5 hurricane on record to strike the island nation.

Interaction with the mountains of Dominica imparted slight weakening of the hurricane to Category 4; however, once over the Caribbean Sea Maria regained Category 5 intensity.

Additional strengthening took place as the storm tracked northwest toward Puerto Rico. Despite the formation of concentric eye walls—the larger one spanning 25 to 35 mi, 40 to 56 km, and the smaller only 5 mi, 8.0 km, signaling the start of an eye wall replacement cycle. The inner violent core remained undisrupted through the afternoon.

Maria attained its peak intensity around 04:00 UTC on September 20, roughly 30 mi, 45 km, south of St. Croix. Sustained winds reached 175 mph, 280 km/h, and its central pressure bottomed out at 908 mbar, bhPa; 26.85 inHg; this ranks it as the tenth-most intense Atlantic hurricane since reliable records began.

Infrared loop of Hurricane Maria passing St. Croix, Vieques, and land falling on Puerto Rico on the morning of September 20

The hurricane made its closest approach to St. Croix around 05:00 UTC on September 20, passing within 20 mi, 30 km of the island; the storm's outer eye wall lashed the island while the more violent inner eye remained offshore.

Hours later, around 08:00 UTC, the outer eye wall struck Vieques, an island off the eastern coast of Puerto Rico.

By this time, the outer eye became dominant as the inner one decayed, and the eye wall replacement cycle caused Maria to weaken to Category 4 strength.

Maria made landfall just south of Yabucoa, Puerto Rico, around 10:15 UTC with sustained winds of 155 mph, 250 km/h, making it the strongest to hit the island since the 1928 San Felipe Segundo hurricane.

Maria maintained a general west-northwest course across Puerto Rico, emerging over the Atlantic Ocean shortly before 18:00 UTC. Interaction with the mountainous terrain resulted in substantial weakening; sustained winds fell to 110 mph (175 km/h) and the central pressure rose to 957 mars, hPa; 28.26 inHg.

With favorable environmental conditions, Maria steadily reorganized as it moved away from Puerto Rico. A large eye, 45 mi, 75 km, wide, developed with deep convection blossoming around it. Early on September 21, the system regained Category 3 intensity.

Initially, cooler waters stirred up by Hurricane Irma two weeks prior limited Maria's reorganization.

During the afternoon of September 21, 2017, the system traversed the Navidad and Silver banks north of the Dominican Republic; shoaling from the region's shallow waters temporarily interfered with measurements of surface winds.

Convection around the storm's eye deepened and its eye became better defined that night, and the hurricane reached a tertiary peak with sustained winds of 125 mph, 205 km/h.

An increase in southwesterly wind shear prompted gradual weakening of the hurricane, starting with restriction of banding features and later degradation of the eye wall. ate on September 22, 2017, the hurricane turned north-northwest as it reached the western periphery of the ridge previously steering it northwest.

Maria fluctuated in organization throughout September 23, 2017 with its eye periodically clearing and becoming cloud-filled; it maintained Category 3 hurricane strength during this phase.

Despite a decreasing central pressure, the storm finally weakened to Category 2 strength early on September 24, 22017. Hurricane Hunters observed flight-level winds of 116 to 135 mph, 187 to 217 km/h; however, surface wind returns by the NOAA's Stepped-Frequency Microwave Radiometer were only 90 mph, 150 km/h. This indicated below-average mixing down of winds in the air.

By this time, Maria's trajectory shifted almost due north between the ridge and a cut-off low over the eastern Gulf of Mexico.

Weakening accelerated later September 24 into September 25, as the hurricane traversed a cold wake with sea surface temperatures of 75–77 °F, 24–25 °C, created by Hurricane Jose a week prior. Maria degraded to Category 1 strength during this time.

Early on September 25, 2017, Maria's structure changed dramatically as its inner core collapsed. The low-level circulation became exposed to the northwest, and most of the deep convection shifted to the eastern half of the storm.

Maria further weakened into a tropical storm during the late afternoon of September 26. However, a sustained convective burst resulted in Maria's winds increasing to hurricane-force once again on September 27, 2017, with banding features evident on the eastern part of the circulation.

Despite this, northwesterly wind shear continued to impinge on the storm, and Maria once again weakened to a tropical storm early on September 28, 2017.

Concurrently, Maria began to accelerate to the east-northeast as it became embedded into the mid-latitude westerlies. Gradually weakening, Maria soon began to move over sea surface temperatures of 73 °F, 23 °C, and below, causing most of its convection to dissipate. Late on September 30, Maria transitioned into an extra tropical cyclone.

During the next couple of days, Maria's artifact accelerated towards the United Kingdom, while rapidly weakening. Maria's remnants later crossed the Iberian Peninsula into the western Mediterranean Sea on October 3, before being absorbed by another frontal system later the same day.

The U.S. Navy helps evacuate military personnel from the U.S. Virgin Islands, ahead of Hurricane Maria.

Upon the initiation of the National Hurricane Center, NHC's, first advisories for the system that would become Tropical Storm Maria on the morning of September 16, 2017, the government of France issued tropical storm watches for the islands of Martinique and Guadeloupe, while St. Lucia issued a tropical storm watch for its citizens, and the government of Barbados issued a similar watch for Dominica.

Barbados would later that day declare a tropical storm watch for its citizens and Saint Vincent and the Grenadines.

The government of Antigua and Barbuda issued Hurricane watches for the islands of Antigua, Barbuda, St. Kitts, Nevis, and Montserrat by the time of the NHC's second advisory which declared Maria a tropical storm.

The Dominican Republic activated the International Charter on Space and Major Disasters for humanitarian satellite coverage on the 20th.

Puerto Rico was still recovering from Hurricane Irma two weeks prior, approximately 80,000 remained without power as Maria approached.

Puerto Rico Electric Power Authority, PREPA, struggled with increasing debt, reaching $9 billion even before the hurricanes prompting them to file for bankruptcy.

Furthermore, the company lost 30 percent of its employees since 2012. Aging infrastructure across the island makes the grid more susceptible to damage from storms; the median age of PREPA power plants is 44 years.

Inadequate safety also plagues the company and local newspapers frequently describe poor maintenance and outdated controls.

Evacuation orders were issued in Puerto Rico in advance of Maria, and officials announced that 450 shelters would open in the afternoon of September 18. As of September 19, at least 2,000 people in Puerto Rico had sought shelter.

As Maria approached the coast of North Carolina and threatened to bring tropical storm conditions, a storm surge warning was issued for the coast between Ocracoke Inlet and Cape Hatteras, while a storm surge watch was issued for the Pamlico Sound, the lower Neuse River, and the Alligator River on the morning of September 26, 2017.

A state of emergency was declared by officials in Dare and Hyde counties, while visitors were ordered to evacuate Hatteras and Ocracoke islands.

Ferry service between Ocracoke and Cedar Island was suspended the evening of September 25, and remained suspended on September

26 and 27, due to rough seas, while ferry service between Ocracoke and Hatteras Island was suspended on September 26 and 27.

The port in Morehead City was closed by the United States Coast Guard on the morning of September 26. Schools in Dare County closed on September 26 and 27, while schools in Carteret and Tyrrell counties, along with Ocracoke Island, dismissed early on September 26, in anticipation of high winds. Schools in Currituck County were closed on September 27, 2017, due to high winds.

The outer rain bands of Maria produced heavy rainfall and strong gusts across the southern Windward Islands. The Hewanorra and George F. L. Charles airports of Saint Lucia respectively recorded 4.33 in, 110 mm, and 3.1 in, 80 mm of rain, though even higher quantities fell elsewhere on the island.

Scattered rockslides, landslides and uprooted trees caused minor damage and blocked some roads. Several districts experienced localized blackouts due to downed or damaged power lines. The agricultural sector, especially the banana industry, suffered losses from the winds.

Heavy rainfall amounting to 3–5 in, 75–125 mm, caused scattered flooding across Barbados; in Christ Church, the flood waters trapped residents from the neighborhood of Goodland in their homes and inundated the business streets of Saint Lawrence Gap.

Maria stirred up rough seas that flooded coastal sidewalks in Bridgetown and damaged boats as operators had difficulties securing their vessels.

High winds triggered an island-wide power outage and downed a coconut tree onto a residence in Saint Joseph.

Passing 30 mi, 50 km, off the northern shorelines, Maria brought torrential rainfall and strong gusts to Martinique but spared the island of its hurricane-force wind field, which at the time extended 25 mi, 35 km, around the eye.

The commune of Le Marigot recorded 6.7 inches, 170 mm of rain over a 24-hour period. By September 19, Maria had knocked out power to 70,000 households, about 40% of the population. Water service was cut to 50,000 customers, especially in the communes of Le Morne-Rouge and Gros-Morne.

Numerous roads and streets, especially along the northern coast, were impassible due to rockslides, fallen trees and toppled power poles. Streets in Fort-de-France were inundated.

In the seaside commune of Le Carbet, rough seas washed ashore large rocks and demolished some coastal structures, while some boats were blown over along the bay of the commune of Schœlcher.

Martinique's agricultural sector suffered considerable losses: about 70% of banana crops sustained wind damage, with nearly every tree downed along the northern coast. There were no deaths on the island, although four people were injured in the hurricane, two seriously and two lightly.

An aerial view of part of Roseau, revealing widespread damage to roofs. Flash floods clogged roads with debris—vegetative and structural and mud.

Rainfall ahead of the hurricane caused several landslides in Dominica as water levels across the island began to rise by the afternoon of September 18.

Maria made landfall at 21:15 AST that day, 1:15 UTC, September 19, as a Category 5 hurricane with maximum sustained winds of 160 mph, 260 km/h.

These winds, the most extreme to ever impact the island, battered the roof of practically every home, including the official residence of Prime Minister Roosevelt Skerrit, who required rescue when his home began to flood.

Downing all cellular, radio and internet services, Maria effectively cut Dominica off from the outside world; the situation there remained unclear for a couple of days after the hurricane's passage.

Skerrit called the devastation "mind boggling" before going offline, and indicated immediate priority was to rescue survivors rather than assess damage. Initial ham radio reports from the capital of Roseau on September 19, 20`7 indicated "total devastation," with half the city flooded, cars stranded, and stretches of residential area "flattened".

The next morning, the first aerial footage of Dominica elucidated the scope of the destruction. Maria left the mountainous country blanketed in a field of debris: Rows of houses along the entirety of the coastline were rendered uninhabitable, as widespread floods and landslides littered neighborhoods with the structural remnants.

The hurricane also inflicted extensive damage to roads and public buildings, such as schools, stores, and churches, and affected all of Dominica's 73,000 residents in some form or way.

The air control towers and terminal buildings of the Cranefield and Douglas Charles airports were severely damaged, although the runways remained relatively intact and open to emergency landings.

The disaster affected all the island's 53 health facilities, including the badly damaged primary hospital, compromising the safety of many patients.

A road in the Roseau area is littered with structural debris, damaged vegetation and downed power poles and lines.

The infrastructure of Roseau was left in ruins; practically every power pole and line were downed, and the main road was reduced to fragments of flooded asphalt.

The winds stripped the public library of its roof panels and demolished all but one wall of the Baptist church. To the south of Roseau, riverside flooding and numerous landslides impacted the town of Pointe Michel, destroying about 80% of its structures and causing most of the deaths in the country.

Outside the capital area, the worst of the destruction was concentrated around the east coast and rural areas, where collapsed roads and bridges isolated many villages. The port and fishing town of Marigot, Saint Andrew Parish, was 80% damaged.

Settlements in Saint David Parish, such as Castle Bruce, Good Hope and Grand Fond, had been practically eradicated; many homes hung off cliffs or decoupled from their foundations.

In Rosalie, rushing waters gushed over the village's bridge and damaged facilities in its bay area. Throughout Saint Patrick Parish, the extreme winds ripped through roofs and scorched the vegetation.

Buildings in Grand Bay, the parish's main settlement, experienced total roof failure or were otherwise structurally compromised. Many houses in La Plaine caved in or slid into rivers, and its single bridge was broken.

Overall, the hurricane damaged the roofs of as much as 98% of the island's buildings, including those serving as shelters; half of the houses had their frames destroyed. Its ferocious winds defoliated nearly all vegetation, splintering or uprooting thousands of trees and decimating the island's lush rainforests.

The agricultural sector, a vital source of income for the country, was completely wiped out: 100% of banana and tuber plantations was lost, as well as vast amounts of livestock and farm equipment.

In Maria's wake, Dominica's population suffered from an island-wide water shortage due to uprooted pipes. The Caribbean Disaster Emergency Management Agency, CDEMA, estimates that the hurricane has caused "billions of dollars" worth of damage. As of October 9, there are 28 fatalities confirmed across the island, with another 32 people reported missing.

Numerous trees fell across Guadeloupe, clogging roadways with debris

Blustery conditions spread over Guadeloupe as Maria tracked to the south of the archipelago, which endured hours of unbaiting hurricane-force winds.

The strongest winds blew along the southern coastlines of Basse-Terre Island: Gourbeyre observed a peak wind speed of 101 mph, 162 km/h, while winds up north in nearby Baillif reached 92 mph, 148 km/h.

Along those regions, the hurricane kicked up extremely rough seas with 20 ft., 6 m, waves.

The combination of rough seas and winds was responsible for widespread structural damage and flooding throughout the archipelago, especially from Pointe-à-Pitre, along Grand-Terre Island's southwestern coast, to Petit-Bourg and the southern coasts on Basse-Terre Island.

Aside from wind-related effects, rainfall from Maria was also significant. In just a day, the hurricane dropped nearly a month's worth of rainfall at some important locations: Pointe-à-Pitre recorded a 24-hour total of 7.5 inches, 191 mm, while the capital of Basse-Terre measured 6.4 in, 163 mm.

Even greater quantities fell at higher elevations of Basse Terre Island, with a maximum total of 18.07 in, 459 mm, measured at the mountainous locality of Matouba, Saint-Claude.

Throughout the archipelago, the hurricane left 40% of the population, 80,000 households, without power and 25% of landline users without service. The islands of Marie-Galante, La Désirade and especially Les Saintes bore the brunt of the winds, which caused heavy damage to structures and nature alike and cut the islands off from their surroundings for several days.

Homes on Terre-de-Haut Island of Les Saintes were flooded or lost their roofs. On the mainland, sections of Pointe-à-Pitre stood under more than 3.3 feet, 1 m of water, and the city's hospital sustained significant damage. The Basse-Terre region suffered severe damage to nearly 100% of its banana crops, comprising a total area of more than 5,000 acres, 2,000 hectares; farmers described the destruction to their plantations as "complete annihilation".

Beyond their impact on farmland, the strong winds ravaged much of the island's vegetation fallen trees and branches covered practically every major road and were responsible for one death.

Another person was killed upon being swept out to sea. Two people disappeared at sea after their vessel capsized offshore La Désirade, east of mainland Grande-Terre. Damage from Maria across Guadeloupe amounted to at least €100 million, US$120 million.

Maria's outer eye wall was reported by the National Hurricane Center to have crossed Saint Croix while the hurricane was at Category 5 intensity.

The hurricane caused extensive and severe damage to the island. Sustained winds at the Sandy Point National Wildlife Refuge reached 99 to 104 mph, 159 to 167 km/h, and gusted to 137 mph, 220 km/h.

The Luis Hospital suffered roof damage and flooding but remained operational. One person died from a storm-induced heart attack.

The storm made landfall on Puerto Rico on Wednesday, September 20. A sustained wind of 64 mph, 103 km/h, with a gust to 113 mph, 182 km/h, was reported in San Juan, Puerto Rico, immediately prior to the hurricane making landfall on the island.

After landfall, wind gusts of 109 mph, 175 km/h, were reported at Yabucoa Harbor and 118 mph, 190 km/h, at Camp Santiago.

In addition, very heavy rainfall occurred throughout the territory, peaking at 37.9 in, 962.7 mm, in Caguas.

Widespread flooding affected San Juan, waist-deep in some areas, and numerous structures lost their roof. The coastal La Perla neighborhood of San Juan was largely destroyed.

Cataño saw extensive damage, with the Juana Matos neighborhood estimated to be 80 percent destroyed. The primary airport in San Juan, the Luis Muñoz Marín International Airport, was slated to reopen on September 22, 2017.

Storm surge and flash flooding stemming from flood gate releases at La Plata Lake Dam converged on the town of Toa Baja, trapping thousands of residents. Survivors indicate that flood waters rose at least 6 ft, 1.8 m, in 30 minutes, with flood waters reaching a depth of 15 ft, 4.6 m, in some areas.

More than 2,000 people were rescued once military relief reached the town 24 hours after the storm. At least eight people died due to the flooding while many are unaccounted for. There were 117 people missing.

On September 24, 2017, Governor Rosselló estimated that the damage from Hurricane Maria in Puerto Rico was surely over the $8 billion damage by Hurricane Georges.

Approximately 80 percent of the territory's agriculture was lost due to the hurricane, with agricultural losses estimated at $780 million.

The hurricane destroyed the island's power grid, leaving all 3.4 million residents without electricity. Puerto Rican governor Ricardo Rosselló stated that it could take months to restore power in some locations, with San Juan Mayor Carmen Yulín Cruz estimating that some areas would remain without power for four to six months.

Communication networks were crippled across the island. Ninety-five percent of cell networks were down with 48 of the island's 78 counties networks being completely inoperable.

Eighty-five per cent of above-ground phone and internet cables were knocked out. Only one radio station, WAPA 680 AM, remained on-air through the storm.

The NEXRAD Doppler weather radar of Puerto Rico has also been literally blown away. The radome which covers the radar antenna, and which had to withstand winds of more than 130 mph, was destroyed while the antenna of 30 feet in diameter was blown from the pedestal, the latter remaining intact.

The radar is 2800 feet above sea level and the anemometer at the site measured winds of about 145 mph before communications broke, which means winds at that height were likely 20 percent higher than what was seen at sea level. Its replacement will take a few months.

The nearby island of Vieques suffered similarly extensive damage. Communications were largely lost across the island. Widespread property destruction

The recreational ship Ferrell carrying a family of four issued a distress signal while battling 20 ft, 6.1 m, seas and 115 mph. 185 km/h, winds on September 20, 2017.

Communications with the vessel were lost near Vieques on September 20. The United States Coast Guard, United States Navy, and British Royal Navy conducted search-and-rescue operations utilizing an HC-130 aircraft, a fast response cutter, USS Kearsarge, RFA Mounts Bay and Navy helicopters.

On September 21, the mother and her two children were rescued while the father drowned inside the capsized vessel.

Maria's Category 4 winds broke a 96-foot, 29 m, line feed antenna of the Arecibo Observatory, causing it to fall 500 feet, 150 m, and puncturing the dish below, greatly reducing its ability to function until repairs can be made.

Torrential rains and strong winds impacted the Dominican Republic as Maria tracked northeast of the country. Assessments on September 22 indicate 110 homes were destroyed, 570 were damaged, and 3,723 were affected by flooding.

Approximately 60,000 people lost power in northern areas of the country. Flooding and landslides rendered many roads impassable, cutting off 38 communities.

Five people, all of them males, were killed in the Dominican Republic: four of them were of Haitian origin, killed when they were swept away by floodwaters; the fifth person was a Dominican man who died in a landslide.

Hurricane Maria center passed 250 km from Haiti northern coast but has received a large amount of rain and suffered some flooding. Three deaths were reported: a 45-year-old man died in the commune of Limbe, in the department of the North, while attempting to cross a flooded river.

Two other people, a woman, and a man were mortally wounded in Cornillon, a small town 40 kilometers east of the capital Port-au-Prince, according to the authorities.

Maria brushed the Outer Banks of North Carolina on September 26 as the center of the storm passed by offshore and brought tropical storm conditions to the area along with a storm surge, large waves, and rip currents to the coast.

The storm knocked out power to 800 Duke Energy Progress customers in the Havelock area, with restoration of power expected to take several hours.

Dominion North Carolina Power and Cape Hatteras Electric Cooperative experienced scattered power outages. Winds of 23 mph, 37 km/h, and gusts of 41 mph, 66 km/h, were reported at Dare County Regional Airport at Manteo on September 27 while winds of 40 mph, 64 km/h, were reported in Duck.

Maria caused beach erosion at the ferry terminal at the north end of Ocracoke Island that washed out a portion of the paved lanes where vehicles wait to board the ferry.

By the morning of September 26, the storm flooded North Carolina Highway 12 along the coast.

Rip currents from Maria caused three swimmers to drown and several others to be rescued at the Jersey Shore on the weekend of September 23–24. A fourth drowning death occurred in Fernandina Beach, Florida.

In the wake of the hurricane, more than 85% of the island's houses were damaged, of which more than 25% were destroyed, leaving more than 50,000 of the island's 73,000 residents displaced.

Following the destruction of thousands of homes, most supermarkets, and the water supply system, many of Dominica's residents were in dire need of food, water, and shelter for days.

With no access to electricity or running water, and with sewage systems destroyed, fears of widespread diarrhea and dysentery arose....

The island's agriculture, a vital source of income for many, was obliterated as most trees were flattened. Meanwhile, the driving force of the economy and tourism were expected to be scarce in the months that followed Maria.

Prime Minister Roosevelt Skerrit characterized the devastation wrought by Irma and Maria as a sign of climate change and the threat it poses to the survival of his country, stating, "To deny climate change... is to deny a truth we have just lived. "Many islanders suffered respiratory problems because of excessive dust borne out of debris. Light rainfall in the weeks following Maria alleviated this problem, though it also slowed recovery efforts, particularly rebuilding damaged rooftops.

Through the Caribbean Catastrophe Risk Insurance Facility, Dominica received approximately US$19.2 million in emergency funds. USS Wasp, previously deployed to Saint Martin to assist in relief efforts after Hurricane Irma, arrived in Dominica on September 22. The vessel carried two Sikorsky SH-60 Seahawk helicopters to assist in distribution of relief supplies in hard-to-reach areas.

At the United Nations General Assembly on September 23, Prime Minister Roosevelt Skerrit called the situation in Dominica an "international humanitarian emergency". The Royal Canadian Navy vessel HMCS St. John's was dispatched to Dominica at the request of Dominican Prime Minister Skerrit.

The prime minister urged churches to encourage their membership to provide housing for senior citizens and disabled, many of whom remained in damaged structures despite tarpaulin donations from Venezuela, Palestine, Cuba, Jamaica, and other countries.

As schools began to reopen on October 16, the United Nations Children's Fund reported that the entire child population of Dominica, 23,000 children, remained in danger due to restricted access to clean drinking water.

There's a humanitarian emergency here in Puerto Rico... This is an event without precedent.

The power grid was effectively destroyed by the hurricane, leaving millions without electricity. Governor Ricardo Rosselló estimated that Maria caused at least US$ 90 billion in damage.

As of September 26, 2017, 95% of the island was without power, less than half the population had potable water, and 95% of the island had no cell phone service.

On October 6, 20217, a little more than two weeks after the hurricane, 89% still had no power, 44% had no water service, and 58% had no cell service.

One month after the hurricane, 88% of the island was without power, about 3 million people, 29% lacked potable water, about 1 million people, and 40% of the island had no cell service.

All hospitals were open, but most were on backup generators that provide limited power. About half of sewage treatment plants on the island were not functioning.

FEMA reported 60,000 homes needed roofing help and had distributed 38,000 roofing tarps.

The island's highways and bridges remained heavily damaged nearly a month later. Only 392 miles of Puerto Rico's 5,073 miles of road were open. Some towns continue to be isolated and delivery of relief supplies including food and water are hampered—helicopters are the only alternative.

As of October 1, 2017, there were ongoing fuel shortage and distribution problems, with 720 of 1,100 gas

The Guajataca Dam was structurally damaged, and on September 22, 2017, the National Weather Service issued a flash flood emergency for parts of the area in response.

Tens of thousands of people were ordered to evacuate the area, with about 70,000 thoughts to be at risk.

The entirety of Puerto Rico was declared a Federal Disaster Zone shortly after the hurricane. The Federal Emergency Management Agency planned to open an air bridge with three to four aircraft carrying essential supplies to the island daily starting on September 22.

Beyond flights involving the relief effort, limited commercial traffic resumed at Luis Muñoz Marín International Airport on September 22 under primitive conditions.

A dozen commercial flights operated daily as of September 26. By October 3, there were 39 commercial flights per day from all Puerto Rican airports, about a quarter of the normal number.

The next day, airports were reported to be operating at normal capacity. In marked contrast to the initial relief efforts for Hurricane Katrina and the 2010 Haiti earthquake, on September 22, the only signs of relief efforts were besieged Puerto Rican government employees.

The territory's government contracted 56 small companies to assist in restoring power. Eight FEMA Urban Search & Rescue, US&R, teams were deployed to assist in rescue efforts.

On September 24, 2017, the amphibious assault ship USS Kearsarge, and the dock landing ship USS Oak Hill under Rear Admiral Jeffrey W. Hughes along with the 2,400 marines of 26th Marine Expeditionary Unit arrived to assist in relief efforts.

By September 24, 2017, there were 13 United States Coast Guard ships deployed around Puerto Rico assisting in the relief and restoration efforts: the National Security Cutter USCGC James; the medium endurance cutters USCGC Diligence, USCGC Forward, USCGC Venturous, and USCGC Valiant; the fast response cutters USCGC Donald Horsley, USCGC Heriberto Hernandez, USCGC Joseph Napier, USCGC Richard Dixon, and USCGC Winslow Griesser; the coastal patrol boat USCGC Yellow fin; and the seagoing buoy tenders USCGC Cypress and USCGC Elm.

Federal aid arrived on September 25 with the reopening of major ports. Eleven cargo vessels collectively carrying 1.3 million liters of water, 23,000 cots, and dozens of generators arrived.

Full operations at the ports of Guayanilla, Salinas, and Tallaboa resumed on September 25, while the ports of San Juan, Fajardo, Culebra, Guayama, and Vieques had limited operations.

The United States Air Force Air Mobility Command has dedicated eight C-17 Globe master aircraft to deliver relief supplies. The Air Force assisted the Federal Aviation Administration with air traffic control repairs to increase throughput capacity.

The United States Transportation Command has moved additional personnel and eight U.S. Army UH-60 Black Hawk helicopters from

Fort Campbell, Kentucky to Luis Muñoz Marín International Airport to increase distribution capacity.

The United States Army Corps of Engineers deployed 670 personnel engaged in assessing and restoring the power grid; as of September 25, 83 generators were installed, and an additional 186 generators were en route.

As of September 26, 2017, agencies of the U.S. government have delivered 4 million meals, 6 million liters of water, 70,000 tarps and 15,000 rolls of roof sheeting.

National Guard troops were activated and deployed to Puerto Rico from Connecticut, Georgia, and other states.

Members of the South Carolina National Guard assisting with cleanup efforts in Caguas.

On September 26, the hospital ship USNS Comfort prepared to deploy and subsequently arrived a week later in Puerto Rico. However, most of the 250-bed floating state-of-the-art hospital has gone unused despite overburdened island clinics and hospitals.

Puerto Rico's Department of Health is supposed to refer patients there, but there had been few referrals by October 17. Governor Rosselló explained that "The disconnect or the apparent disconnect was in the communications flow" and added "I asked for a complete revision of that so that we can now start sending more patients over there."

On September 27, the Pentagon reopened two major airfields on Puerto Rico and started sending aircraft, specialized units, and a hospital ship to assist in the relief effort.

Brigadier General Richard C. Kim, the deputy commanding general of United States Army North, will be responsible for coordinating operations between the military, FEMA and other government agencies, and the private sector.

Massive amounts of water, food, and fuel have either been delivered to ports in Puerto Rico or are held up at ports in the mainland United States because there is a lack of trucker drivers to move the goods into the interior. The lack of communication networks has slowed down the effort as only 20% of drivers have reported to work.

As of September 28, the Port of San Juan has only been able to dispatch 4% of deliveries received. There has been very little room to accept additional shipments.

As of September 28, 2017, 44 percent of the population was without drinking water. The U.S. military is shifting from "a short term, sea-based response to a predominantly land-based effort designed to provide robust, longer-term support" with fuel delivery a top priority.

A joint Army National Guard and Marine expeditionary unit team established an Installation Staging Base at the former Roosevelt Roads Naval Station. They <u>transported</u> via helicopter Department of Health and Human Services assessment teams to hospitals across Puerto Rico to determine medical requirements.

On September 29,2017, the amphibious assault ship USS Wasp which was providing relief activities to the island of Dominica was diverted to Puerto Rico.

As of September 30, 2017, FEMA official Alejandro de la Campa stated that 5% of electricity, 33% of the telecommunications infrastructure, and 50% of water services was restored to the island.

More than a week after Hurricane Maria struck, residents of Ponce, Puerto Rico wait in long lines at an ATM to withdraw cash. I recalled that my dad and I were waiting to get some cash from the ATM. When it was our turn to withdraw money, there was nothing.

We were informed that we must return the next day. The sad part was that we needed food and water. The supermarket didn't have access to ATM. The only people that could shop were food stamp recipients and those with cash. We had none....

On September 28, 2017, Lieutenant General Jeffrey S. Buchanan was dispatched to Puerto Rico to lead all military hurricane relief efforts there and to see how the military can be more effective in the recovery effort, particularly in dealing with the thousands of containers of supplies that are stuck in port because of "red tape, lack of drivers, and a crippling power outage".

On September 29, 2017, Jeffrey S, Buchanan stated that there were not enough troops and equipment in place, but more would be arrived soon.

With centralized fossil-fuel-based power plants and grid infrastructure expected to be out of commission for weeks to months, some renewable energy projects are in the works, including the <u>shipment of hundreds of Tesla Powerwall battery systems to be</u> integrated with solar PV systems and Sonnen solar microgrid projects at 15 emergency community centers, the first expected to be completed in October.

In addition, other solar companies jumped into help, including Sunnova and New Start Solar. A charity called Light Up Puerto Rico raised money to both purchase and deliver solar products, including solar panels, on Oct. 19, 2017.

Many TV and movie stars are donating money to hurricane relief organizations to help the victims of Harvey and Maria. Prominently, Jennifer Aniston has pledged a million U.S. dollars, dividing the amount equally between the Red Cross and The Ricky Martin Foundation for Puerto Rico. Martin's foundation had raised over three million dollars as of October 13, 2017.

On October 10, 2017, Carnival Cruise Lines announced that it would resume departures of cruises from San Juan on October 15, 2017.

On October 13, 2017, both CNN and The Guardian reported that Puerto Ricans are drinking water being pumped from a well at an EPA Superfund site; the water was later determined to be safe to drink.

On October 13, 2017, the Trump administration requested $4.9 billion to fund a loan program that Puerto Rico can use to address basic functions and infrastructure needs.

As of October 20, 2017, only 18.5% of the island had electricity, 49.1% of cell towers were working, and 69.5% of customers had running water, with the slowest restoration in the north.

Ports and commercial flights were back to normal operations, but 7.6% of USPS locations, 11.5% of supermarkets, and 21.4% of gas stations were still closed.

There were 4,246 people still living in emergency shelters, and tourism was down by half.

Standing water in Ponce, Puerto Rico more than a week after Hurricane Maria hit the island…

A possible outbreak of leptospirosis affected survivors in the weeks following the hurricane. The bacterial infection spreads through unsanitary water, often with contaminated animal urine. With large areas of Puerto Rico lacking clean water, residents were forced to use contaminated sources of water.

As of October 23, 2017, at least 4 people died from the disease while 74 others are suspected of being infected. Despite the possibility of an outbreak, officials have not ed the situation as such.

On October 24, 2017, the number of deaths in Puerto Rico blamed on Hurricane Maria has increased to 51 with officials saying two more people died from leptospirosis in contaminated water.

On October 5, 2017, NPR reported an additional 49 bodies unidentified. The cause of death sent to a hospital morgue was contaminated water.

The Los Angeles Times reported 50 more deaths than normal in one region in the three days after the hurricane. Puerto Rico's Center for Investigative Reporting reported 69 hospital morgues are at "capacity." Exact figure is unknown.

According to El Vocero newspaper, 350 bodies are being stored at the Institute of Forensic Sciences. Many bodies were awaiting autopsies.

In the report, Héctor Pesquera, secretary of the Puerto Rico Department of Public Safety, did not say how many, if any, of the cadavers were there before the storm.

On October 11, 2017, Vox reported 81 deaths directly or indirectly related to the hurricane with another 450 deaths awaiting investigation. Furthermore, they indicated 69 people to be missing.

On October 14, 2-17, CNN reported the number of missing people to be about 117. In a message to the DHS, Representatives Nydia Velazquez and Bennie Thompson wrote, "It would be morally reprehensible to intentionally underreport the true death toll to portray relief efforts as more successful than they are."

Between September 20, 2017, and October 18,201, the island's only medical examiner authorized 911 bodies for cremation. The cause of death for the persons are listed as "natural causes".

Soon after the hurricane struck, Whitefish Energy, a small Montana-based company with only two full-time employees, was awarded a $300 million contract by PREPA to repair Puerto Rico's power grid.

The company contracted more than 300 personnel and sent them to the island to carry out work. PREPA cited Whitefish's comparatively small upfront cost of $3.7 million for mobilization as one of the main reasons for contracting them over larger companies.

PREPA Executive Director Ricardo Ramos stated:

"Whitefish was the only company—it was the first that could be mobilized to Puerto Rico. It did not ask us to be paid soon or a guarantee to pay". No requests for assistance were made to the American Public Power Association by October 24, 2017.

The decision to hire such a tiny company was considered highly unusual by many, such as former Energy Department official Susan Tierney, who stated:

"The fact that there are so many utilities with experience in this and a huge track record of helping each other out, it is at least odd why the utility would go to Whitefish".

As the company was based in Whitefish, Mont., the hometown of US Interior Secretary Ryan Zinke, this also led to accusations of privatization, though Zinke dismissed these claims and stated that he had no role in securing the contract.

Several representatives, both Democrats and Republicans, also voiced their concern over the choice to contract Whitefish instead of other companies.

In a press release on October 27, 2017, FEMA stated it did not approve of PREPA's contract with Whitefish and cited "significant concerns". Governor Rosselló subsequently ordered an audit of the contract's budget.

DHS Inspector General John Roth led the FEMA audit while Governor Rosselló called for a second review by Puerto Rico's Office of Management and Budget.

As of September 25, 2017, the U.S. Coast Guard reports that the ports of Crown Bay, East Gregerie Channel, West Gregerie Channel, and Redbook Bay on Saint Thomas; the ports of Krause Lagoon, Limetree Bay, and Frederiksted on Saint Croix, and the port of Cruz Bay on Saint John are open with restrictions.

On September 25, 2017, 11 flights arrived with 200,000 meals, 144,000 liters of water, and tarps. Troops have been activated and deployed to the U.S. Virgin Islands from the Virginia National Guard, the West Virginia National Guard, Missouri National Guard. UH-60 Blackhawk helicopters from the Tennessee Army National Guard.

Nearly a month after the hurricane, only 16 percent of people in St. Thomas and 1.6 percent of people in St. Croix have had electricity restored.

The U.S. Department of Homeland Security did not immediately waive the Jones Act for Puerto Rico. It prevented the commonwealth from receiving any aid and supplies from non-U.S.-flagged vessels from U.S. ports.

The waiver was granted after two days, while in contrast the waiver was not granted for Hurricane Harvey until fourteen days after the hurricane and was narrowly drafted to only allow fuel transportation for seven days.

A DHS Security spokesman said that there would be enough U.S. shipping for Puerto Rico, and that the limiting factors would be port capacity and local transport capacity. This statement was supported by AFL/CIO which issued a "fact checking" statement regarding the Jones Act and its effect upon recovery relief.

The Jones Act was waived for a period of ten days starting on September 28, 2017, following a formal request by Puerto Rico Governor Rosselló.

San Juan Mayor Carmen Yulín Cruz, called the disaster a "terrifying humanitarian crisis" and pleaded for relief efforts to be sped up on September 26 the White House contested claims that the administration was not responding effectively.

General Joseph L. Lengyel, Chief of the National Guard Bureau, defended the Trump Administration's response, and reiterated that relief efforts were obstructed by Puerto Rico being an island rather than on the mainland.

## President Donald Trump responded to accusations that he does not care about Puerto Rico:

"Puerto Rico is very important to me, and Puerto Rico—the people are fantastic people. I grew up in New York, so I know many people from Puerto Rico. I know many Puerto Ricans. And these are great people, and we must help them. The island is devastated." Frustrated with the federal government's "slow and inadequate response", relief group Oxfam announced on October 2, 2017, that it plans to get involved in the humanitarian aid effort, sending a team to "assess a targeted and effective response" and support its local partners' on-the-ground efforts.

On October 2, 2017, Oxfam released a rare statement; "While the US government is engaged in relief efforts, it has failed to address the most urgent needs.

Oxfam has monitored the response in Puerto Rico closely, and we are outraged at the slow and inadequate response the US Government has mounted," said Oxfam America's president Abby Maxman. "Oxfam rarely responds to humanitarian emergencies in the US and other wealthy countries, but as the situation in Puerto Rico worsens and the federal government's response continues to falter, we have decided to step in.

The U.S. has more than enough resources to mobilize an emergency response but has failed to do so in a swift and robust manner." In an update on October 19, the agency called the situation in Puerto Rico "unacceptable" and called for "a more robust and efficient response from the U.S. government".

On October 3, 2017, President Trump visited Puerto Rico. He compared the damage from Hurricane Maria to that of Hurricane Katrina, saying:

"If you looked, every death is a horror, but if you look at a real catastrophe like Katrina, and you look at the tremendous hundreds and hundreds and hundreds of people that died, and you look at what happened here with really a storm that was just totally overbearing, nobody has seen anything like this.

What is your death count as of this morning, 17?". Trump's remarks were widely criticized for implying that Hurricane Maria was not a "real catastrophe".

While in Puerto Rico, Trump also distributed canned goods and paper towels to crowds gathered at a relief shelter and told the residents of the devastated island "I hate to tell you, Puerto Rico, but you've thrown our budget a little out of whack, because we've spent a lot of money on Puerto Rico, and that's fine. We saved a lot of lives."

On October 12, 2017, Trump tweeted, "We cannot keep FEMA, the Military & the First Responders, who have been amazing, under the most difficult circumstances in P.R. forever!", prompting further criticism from lawmakers in both parties]; Mayor Cruz replied, "You are incapable of empathy and frankly simply cannot get the job done."

In response to a request for clarification on the tweet from Governor Rosselló, John F. Kelly assured that no resources were being pulled and replied: "Our country will stand with those American citizens in Puerto Rico until the job is done".

A review of several estimates measuring the costs of the damage that Hurricane Maria bent on Puerto Rico when it slammed the island on Sept. 20, 2017, reveals wide variations from a high of $95 billion by Moody's Analytics to a low of $15.9 billion by Estudios Técnicos.

"While it remains too early for us to provide a damage assessment, a preliminary report from Moody's Analytics suggested it could be approximately $95 billion, which is roughly 150% of Puerto Rico's annual GNP [gross national product," said the island's Financial Oversight Management Board in a letter to Congress dated Oct. 3, 2017. "The FOMB urges Congress to heed the Governor's calls for the maximum federal assistance to Puerto Rico in order to help it respond to and recover from Hurricanes Irma and Maria."

The $95 billion mark includes "lost output" and infrastructure damages.

According to a preliminary Oct. 1 report to the Puerto Rico Manufacturers Association, ET estimates total damages from Maria at between $15.9 billion to $19.9 billion. Infrastructure damages range from $14.9 billion to $18.6 billion, while economic damages range from $1 billion to $1.3 billion.

Chuck Watson, an analyst with the disaster research group Enki Research, puts total damages at $30 billion, which includes $20 billion in physical damages and $10 billion in lost economic productivity, according to CNN. money.

Meanwhile, AIR Worldwide, a catastrophe modeling firm, "estimates industry insured losses for Hurricane Maria in the Caribbean will be between $40 billion and $85 billion. Puerto Rico alone accounts for more than 85% of the loss," noting that hurricanes Irma and Maria have been major catastrophes for the Caribbean. An analysis of the numbers for Maria show discrepancies around economic damages.

Estudios Técnicos' numbers for infrastructure damage and economic damages, which measures the relationship between the two, are at 14 to 1. Watson's numbers put the ratio at 2 to 1. Watson's numbers are like a 1999 Planning Board report on Hurricane Georges, which hit the island in 1998.

That Planning Board report put total damages at $4.3 billion, including $2.85 billion in infrastructure damages and $1.4 billion in economic damages. Therefore, this ratio is also at 2 to 1.

Based on this analysis, Estudios Técnicos' ratio seems to be very low.

Moreover, Estudios Técnicos' high-end estimate for economic damages from Maria, $1.3 billion, is lower than the Planning Board's number of $1.4 billion for Georges. Given the widespread destruction that Maria has wreaked on Puerto Rico, $1.3 billion in economic damages also seems to be very low.

# CHAPTER 8

## Progress still stalled four years after Hurricane Maria

The memories of surviving Hurricane Maria still haunt me. I live in Puerto Rico, and I went through those horrible hours during the hurricane. It has been four years after the storm created chaos in our island on Sept. 20, 2017. I don't see that much improvement on fixing the damages created by the hurricane.

There are reminders of the destruction. There still thousands of homes, many of them still covered with blue tarps. Constant power outages remind Puerto Ricans that essential work to modernize the antiquated electric grid decimated by Maria has not yet begun.

Deteriorating school buildings, roads, bridges and even health care facilities point to a slow reconstruction process that has not yet picked up its pace.

A new analysis by the Center for a New Economy, a Puerto Rico-based nonpartisan think tank, argues that rebuilding after the hurricane is just one of three "systemic shocks". This goes along with the Covid-19 pandemic and the decadelong financial crisis that is challenging Puerto Rico.

Concerning reconstruction, some of the most important work, which includes "undertaking improvement activities to increase the ability and reduce the risk exposure of the weak populations has not yet begun," according to the analysis.

"If a hurricane today, category one, hits the island, it will not survive. The power grid will not survive," Rep. Nydia Velázquez, D-N.Y., said during a press conference Monday hosted by the Hispanic Federation to remember the roughly 3,000 lives that were lost to Hurricane Maria.

Puerto Ricans are experiencing blackouts almost daily and every single one of those blackouts takes them back to that unforgettable dawn of September 2017," said the congresswoman of Puerto Rican descent. "Thousands of houses with blue tarps. That is happening in America."

Hurricane Maria left $90 billion in damages and Congress allocated at least $63 billion for disaster relief and recovery operations. Four years later, about 71 percent of those funds have not reached communities on the island archipelago. Puerto Rico has received about $18 billion, according to FEMA's Recovery Support Function Leadership Group.

"As we invest in upgrading and modernizing our American infrastructure system, we have to make sure that we do it everywhere, in every community," Sen. Kirsten Gillibrand, D-N.Y., said in the press conference alongside Velázquez. "That starts with ensuring that Puerto Rico's needs are included in the build back better agenda, and that our infrastructure investments meet the greatest need."

The Fiscal Oversight and Management Board overseeing Puerto Rico's finances has said the remaining bulk of the reconstruction aid is scheduled to be disbursed after fiscal year 2025, according to Sergio Marxuach, CNE's policy director and author of the analysis.

Created during the Obama administration under the 2016 Promise law, the federal fiscal board is responsible for restructuring Puerto Rico's $72 billion public debt after U.S. laws arbitrarily excluded the U.S. territory from the federal bankruptcy code. It's resulted in tough economy measures as Puerto Rico is trying to jump-start its economic growth.

There are plenty of talk by the government official about the island making it again. I do not see any progress....

Let me tell you that after five weeks after Hurricane Maria, communication was horrible. This is one of my stories that I must tell you.

I haven't heard from my sister. She lives in New York City. I told her once that if she is thinking about me to just look at the sky.

It was about 7 pm November 7, 2017. I miss talking to my sister. My father and I were sitting on the porch drinking coffee. It was very dark; however, the moon was very bright. I started talking to the moon. My dad thought that I was going crazy. I wasn't. I told the moon to please give my sister a sign that we were ok. I kept talking the started getting bigger and brighter....

Month later my sister finally got through us. I received her call. She told me how the moon lit up her whole house. It was just for a moment, and she understood that we were safe...

# CHAPTER 9

# Earthquakes

Aside from hurricanes, tornados, floating etc. we get lots of earthquakes....

## Let's look at the town of GUAYANILLA, Puerto Rico.

This is the story of Gilberto Feliciano. He planned to stay here in the government. He will try to run outdoor shelter. Gilberto was living for three weeks, along with 700 other displaced Puerto Ricans. There were numerous of earthquakes throughout the island. It was very scarry. Gilberto wanted to stay with his people "until the shaking stops."

Gilberto Feliciano's neighborhood is in, Indios, in the islands southwest. It was at the epicenter of back-to-back earthquakes. The earthquakes triggered a string of seismic activity that lasted a month, according to the U.S. Geological Survey.

The first quake, at 5.8 magnitude on Jan. 6, hit as people were celebrating Three Kings Day. The tremor knocked down a popular tourist landmark known as Punta Ventana, on the beach in Guayanilla.

Hours later, a 6.4-magnitude quake, the biggest on the island in a century, destroyed most of Feliciano's hometown. It also killed at least one person, caused an island wide blackout, and devastated countless buildings. It caused $110 million in damages across 559 structures, according to Puerto Rico Gov. Wanda Vázquez.

For Feliciano and over 4,000 other people displaced by the quakes, returning to a safe home is getting more difficult as the U.S. territory's government runs up against funding delays, shortages of inspectors to assess damages, and lack of a viable plan to temporarily relocate those sleeping outdoors to safer housing.

Feliciano, a former construction worker, is convinced that no building in the southern part of Puerto Rico is safe. "My house, especially, moves like a snake. First, you hear a sound like a truck and then the shaking."

Sixteen southern towns hit by the quake have been federally designated as major disaster zones, including Guánica, Guayanilla, Penuelas, Ponce and Yauco. The mayors of those towns estimate that they sustained over $460 million in damages combined.

Angel "Luigi" Torres, the mayor of Yauco, told NBC News that hundreds of small businesses were destroyed in his town and at least 3,261 homes were damaged. Sixty-two of them collapsed and 245 are compromised, meaning that "if it's still trembling, they could fall down."

The road to recovery remains complicated: At least 2,581 quakes have shaken the island this month, according to the Puerto Rico Seismic Network, among them a 5.9-magnitude temblor on Jan.11, a magnitude 5.2 four days later and a magnitude 5.0 this past weekend. At least 186 tremors have been felt on the island, the most in a decade.

People displaced by the quakes share Feliciano's concerns, especially after seeing the unprecedented destruction in their towns.

Mayra Rivera and José Quinones Nazario live in Barrio La Luna in Guánica, where virtually every single home was damaged. They refuse to return until they know it's safe.

The couple put in a request to have government inspectors assess damages and determine whether their house is habitable. Rivera said that the list is so long, no one knows how long it will be before they get answers.

In Yauco, Torres said he's facing the same hurdle because of a shortage of structural engineers trained to inspect damaged infrastructures and determine whether they're safe.

"We have like 40 engineers, but they are not enough," Torres said. "We're in need of engineers that can come here and help us inspect 3,000 homes here that have damages."

Lucy Morales owns one of the collapsed homes in Yauco. Volunteer engineers inspected her house and said it was unsafe. Since then, she's been camping outside her house.

"We've got to stay here because, to get access to the funds from FEMA, the owner has to be here in the house," said Morales, who lives about Alturas del Cafetal, where essentially every single house suffered serious damage.

FEMA Administrator Peter Gaynor told Vázquez on Monday that her administration needs a plan to make sure thousands of people don't live in tents and other outdoor shelters when hurricane season starts in June.

Ayuda Legal Puerto Rico, a nonprofit that provides legal support to low-income communities, is urging Vázquez to release a "temporary and permanent relocation and housing plan" for families who have been living in outdoor shelters "between mud and mosquitoes" and yearn for "decent housing."

Raúl Santiago-Bartolomei, research associate at the Center for a New Economy, a nonpartisan, told NBC News that finding temporary housing may be overwhelming due to an affordable housing crisis that predates 2017's Hurricane Maria, the worst natural disaster in the island's modern history.

Currently, Puerto Rico's limited affordable housing inventory includes about 8,000 homes under the Section 8 housing voucher program and about 20,000 public housing units.

The issue is whether these available housing units are safe, said Ricardo Alvarez-Díaz, an architect who is a governor-appointed member of the Construction and Housing Advisory Council of Puerto Rico.

"Construction codes in Puerto Rico have included seismic requirements since 1987, but much of the buildings were built before then. As a result, many structures and schools are not in compliance," said Álvarez-Díaz, the founder of one of the island's largest architectural firms.

While all the congressionally approved funding for Hurricane Maria complies with seismic code requirements, he said that "more must be done to enforce current construction codes to help ensure the safety of people in Puerto Rico."

Vázquez said at a news conference that the goal is to identify the needs of those who are displaced, brief them on available resources and do the appropriate inspections.

Such resources include the Home Investment Partnership Program, which offers low-income families a chance to buy affordable homes through individual grants or loans.

FEMA's Transitional Sheltering Assistance, which provides short-term lodging to evacuees through hotels or other temporary housing arrangements was granted.

After being hit by Hurricane Maria and the quakes t, it's crucial to "begin to redesign a reconstruction process that allows us to live at low risk, since natural disasters cannot be avoided," said Deepak Lamba-Nieves, a research director at the Center for a New Economy. "Planning is crucial to the mitigation process."

The federal disaster declaration was supposed to allow recovery aid to start flowing to the island to assist thousands of people with temporary housing, home repairs and low-cost loans to cover uninsured property losses, among other kinds of FEMA assistance.

It's still unclear how much aid would go to rebuilding destroyed communities.

House Appropriations Committee Chairwoman Rep. Nita M. Lowey, D-N.Y., introduced legislation to provide $4.67 billion to help Puerto Rico after the earthquakes, but the funding process may face significant delays, just like the disbursement of hurricane relief funds.

The final release of HUD funds also came with a series of last-minute restrictions that severely limit how the money can be used. They seek to prohibit the use of funds to rebuild the island's electrical grid; suspend its $15-an-hour minimum wage for federally funded relief work; require that budget plans be submitted to Puerto Rico's federally appointed fiscal control board; and give more power to a newly appointed federal monitor.

Experts such as Sergio Marxuach, policy director at the Center for a New Economy, worry the restrictions could set a dangerous precedent and disproportionately delay one of the biggest post-disaster reconstructions in U.S. history.

# CHAPTER 10

## Recovery from The Earthquakes

Two years from the series of earthquakes that hit Puerto Rico at the end of 2019, the recovery continues with the help of over $523 million allocated by the Federal Emergency Management Agency, FEMA. The funds are distributed among projects comprising the 14 municipalities of the Southern, Western and Central parts of the island.

Among the structures with most damage because of the earthquakes were the schools on the area, many of which had the "short columns" structural problem, which makes them more vulnerable against seismic events. To repair these and other structural damages on 102 schools, FEMA allocated an additional more than $178.3 million in 2021 to the Department of Education.

"Puerto Rico's history changed because of these earthquakes. As of today, over 518 projects have funds from the agency, mostly for schools and municipalities. We seek to take advantage of this unique opportunity to strengthen the structures where public education is given and additional spaces within the affected area," said the Federal Disaster Recovery Coordinator, José G. Vaquero.

Schools, public buildings and roads, the efforts include private property debris removal. Over 86 residences in Guánica and Yauco have already been demolished, which will start the long-term recovery of these families.

In this journey towards recovery is Janet Vega Padro, resident of the Esperanza neighborhood in Guánica, who lost her home because of the earthquakes. "The first step has already been taken, which is the demolition," while she added that she expects to begin rebuilding her home with the funds she received from FEMA.

# CHAPTER 11

# The Exodus after Hurricane Maria

A year since Hurricane Maria struck Puerto Rico, the island has suffered many losses: homes and livelihoods, electricity, and clean water, and tragically, nearly 3,000 lives…

Even as the rebuilding effort goes on, another type of loss is taking a growing toll. The loss of some 200,000 residents who've left the island in search of a better life elsewhere. Without these business owners, skilled workers, doctors, teachers, church members, parents and children, Puerto Rico's future looks even more uncertain.

Damarys Perales and her 10-year-old daughter Alahia are reluctantly joining the exodus.

"It hurts me to leave like this," Damarys told CBS News correspondent David Begnaud, who's been covering the impact since the storm hit. But she adds, "I need the change. We need the change."

When the hurricane slammed ashore on September 20, 2017, Damarys and Alahia had to flee in the middle of the night with little more than the clothes on their backs. A mudslide descended on the house where they'd lived for the past four years. They've been staying with Damarys's mother ever since.

"We were without light for nine months," Damarys said. The power didn't come back on until June 16, the day of her daughter's birthday.

Puerto Rico Governor Ricardo Rosselló says he knows how difficult things have been for families like Damarys's.

"It's been a hard recovery process. The level of devastation and the magnitude of Maria is something that was hard to plan for," Rosselló said. He lays some of the blame on the federal bureaucracy, telling CBS News, "Things that take seven days on a normal transaction from FEMA take over 140 days."

"We've done extraordinary things here," counters Federal Disaster Recovery Coordinator Michael Byrne of FEMA. "Was it enough? Obviously not."

While there are some bright spots of hope and progress in the shuttered businesses and abandoned homes that dot the island, government agencies at every level are still struggling, not just to take care of the living, but also to tend to the dead. The forensics center and morgue in San Juan is overwhelmed, with a backlog of bodies stored in refrigerated 18-wheelers.

The head of forensic sciences, Monica Melendez, said her focus is trying to retain enough staff to work through the burgeoning caseload. The day Begnaud visited, there were 330 bodies on site. Since the hurricane, Melendez said they've been receiving about 25 more bodies per week than they handled before, an additional 100 cases per month.

Those figures reflect an uptick in deaths that continued long after the hurricane winds died down. An independent analysis commissioned by the governor of Puerto Rico and conducted by researchers at George Washington University's Milken Institute School of Public Health determined that about 2,975 people died because of Hurricane Maria in Puerto Rico between September 2017 and February 2018.

By law, the pathologists at this morgue can only work 325 cases per year. And despite the great need, the center keeps losing staff to the U.S. mainland.

"We want to employ pathologists, but they don't want to come, because they say the salary's too low," Melendez said. Here they can earn around $75,000 per year, but in the states, depending on their experience, they could make $150,000 to $200,000.

Puerto Rico's problems didn't start with the hurricane. The island, a U.S. territory, has been in danger of an economic crisis since 2004, and its financial troubles began long before that.

Its population declined from a peak of 3.8 million to about 3.5 million, and since Maria hit, that migration has risen into a full-blown exodus, with an estimated 200,000 more residents picking up and leaving for the U.S. mainland.

Since Puerto Rico is a U.S. commonwealth, and its people American citizens, they are free to travel to the states without restrictions.

The exodus is draining the island of the resource most vital to getting back on its feet: its people. Without them, some fear the island will never fully recover.

Damarys Perales worked as an accountant in Puerto Rico's health department, which provides health care services for nearly 1.5 million people. A year after the hurricane, she can no longer afford to wait for recovery efforts to pay off.

"So, the little savings I have and what I could sell from the things I had is what I'm taking with us to be able to start over in Florida," she said. "We have to take advantage of the opportunities in the moment."

One of the factors driving people to leave is the lack of bare-bones necessities like electricity. The storm downed 80 percent of the island's power lines, leading to the largest blackout in American history and the second largest worldwide.

Yanira Belén Cruz started a Twitter campaign calling out the government for its slow response in the hard-hit community of Utuado, where her elderly grandparents live. Month after month they waited for the electricity to come back on, unable even to power their electric wheelchair. A generator kept a single light bulb illuminated overhead and let them run a fan, the freezer, and a TV for a few hours a day.

Puerto Rico Electric Power Authority said the last of its customers were finally reconnected in mid-August 2018, 11 months after the storm. The government's utility agency is bankrupt and has been plagued by scandal and insufficient resources.

It's not just government agencies struggling to stay afloat. As of 2015, Puerto Rico was losing one doctor every day, increasing wait times, and potentially putting patients with special needs at even greater risk.

Damarys says she looks forward to having better access to health benefits for herself and her daughter on the mainland. This means leaving behind her father, who has Alzheimer's disease.

"I try to spend the most time with him... because if something happens to him, it will be hard for me to come to Puerto Rico, to be with the family in that moment," she said. "But, before that, he told me, if your blessings are in the United States, go. Don't stay here for me."

They also must say goodbye to Alahia's school. One of the most obvious signs of the exodus can be seen in the education system. There are 254 schools shuttered, some damaged by the storm, others closed because children have left.

Since the storm, 42,000 kids have disappeared from the rolls; most are believed to have moved to the mainland and are now enrolled there instead.

So far, half of the Puerto Ricans using their American passports to move stateside are under 24 years old. It is a demographic that is the lifeblood of any labor force.

Some young professionals and artists believe this difficult time may be Puerto Rico's best chance to reshape the island for the better.

"We have gotten stronger," Migdalia Luz Barens told us as the group gathered around a table in Old San Juan. "If anyone had a doubt, any doubt, that Puerto Ricans are struggling on their own. This is a country that has been fighting for its freedom forever."

"I like my school a lot. I was there since first grade. I had a lot of friends," Alahia said. But she said teachers as well as students are walking away.

"She's very smart," said Damarys, who believes a good education for Alahia will be the "biggest benefit" of their move. "Florida is a good place to start. ... It's better because it's bilingual. We'll practice and learn English better."

Hurricane Maria, she said, has forced Puerto Ricans to realize they're on their own. Everyone at the table agreed they'd rather be an independent country.

"Puerto Rico is a colony of the United States, so you can't separate that. It's part of, you were born in a colonized country. In the context of Maria, it's about realizing that you're on your own. That your government won't do the work. The country that has colonized your country won't do the work," Barens said.

What about the billions of dollars in federal aid sent to help the island recover?

"A lot of people contributed money towards Puerto Rico and its recovery. Where's the money? When we still have people without power or potable water, for that matter?" Mariangel Gonzales said.

Governor Ricardo Rosselló says part of the problem is that even though the island's residents don't have a voting representative in Congress, Puerto Rico still gets its marching orders from Washington, leaving it powerless to pick up the pieces on its own.

"It's been a long recovery process," he told CBS News. "But there is an opportunity now for a strong rebuild."

"We got assigned $18.5 billion on the supplemental [federal budget] and $2 billion of that goes towards energy, but the rest goes to housing projects, to rebuilding roads, schools and so forth."

Begnaud asked about the brain drain from residents like Damarys deciding to pick up and move: "You've got really intelligent people who are leaving this island. How do you stop that?"

"Well, here's how I plan to stop that. We're going to have a unique opportunity to rebuild and make fundamental changes to Puerto Rico. We're doing that now. We're doing that in energy, we're doing that in housing, we're doing that in our health care model, we have an education reform in Puerto Rico," Rosselló replied. "We're going to be remembered either as those that paved the way to new a Puerto Rico or those that had the opportunity and didn't do anything for it. You know, I will die trying to make sure that Puerto Rico becomes the place where we can have opportunity and access for all."

The governor's plan relies heavily on the billions of dollars the U.S. government has promised. But many residents who've applied for FEMA aid have been denied because, for one reason or another, they've been unable to prove they own their home.

FEMA coordinator Michael Byrne says that by the one-year anniversary of the storm, the agency will have spent $14.2 billion, and the amount will keep on growing over time. That's far short of the $100 billion Rosselló has called for.

"Well, you don't need that $100 billion tomorrow. You need how much you can use deliberately to do the reconstruction effort right now. We just need to set up the programs and then see what we need year-on-year to be able to make sure that we move forward with the reconstruction," Byrne said.

He also defended FEMA's response to the storm, which many have criticized for exacerbating the disaster.

"I don't buy that. First, I think that's just not the right thing to say to the 17,000 people that came here at the beginning and the early stages and spent every minute of every day working to restore and to aid the Commonwealth and the people of the Commonwealth. The 3,100 people I now have that are spending every day working to provide assistance."

Byrne acknowledges, "There were areas of shortfall that we've been honest about, and we've identified and we're going to work to get better."

One year after the hurricane, as Puerto Rico approaches its second decade of recession and faces over $70 billion in debt, dwindling resources and waning hope may be the new normal.

One economist working with the Financial Oversight and Management Board for Puerto Rico predicts that if the island loses another 1 million people, its population will never return to pre-Maria levels, leaving the Commonwealth a shadow of its former self. Based on the current rate of migration, that turning point could happen in as little as 25 years.

Troubling signs are everywhere. Six weeks after our interview, the head of forensic sciences at the morgue, Monica Melendez, resigned. She was the second director to leave in two months.

And as Damarys's moving date approached, she said an emotional farewell to her church community.

"God bless you. We're all passing through difficult situations, but this time I didn't allow my faith to be broken. I continued to where God was sending me. Let me keep growing, as his daughter, to continue being a role model for my daughter. To give me good health, which I need to keep raising my daughter, and continue forward. Don't let go. I will not forget about you all."

# CHAPTER 12

## Three years Four disasters in Puerto Rico

After Hurricane Maria devastated Puerto Rico, social worker Erica Colón Ortega organized psychologists, therapists, and religious counselors to meet with residents in her community of Dorado.

Many living there had lost all their possessions after floodwater rushed into homes sitting along the river. As Colón Ortega talked to residents about their losses, she also heard about the emotional toll. She could see feelings of despair, sadness, and anguish as they struggled to rebuild.

Now, as COVID-19 rises, mental-health needs in Dorado and across Puerto Rico are further mounting, she and other experts warn. Colón Ortega and other social workers are trying to help, but they say their efforts fall short because they're not officially recognized as disaster-response workers.

Puerto Rico has about 6,000 social workers at government agencies and nonprofit organizations, according to federal estimates. They're charged with helping the most powerless and vulnerable, and during a crisis, they coordinate temporary housing, get help for children in dangerous living conditions, distribute food to the elderly and connect people with legal assistance.

They're also among the first to respond to disaster mental-health needs, from anxiety and sleeplessness to post-traumatic stress. There's been far too much to do since 2017: Hurricane Irma followed by Maria, earthquakes and then the coronavirus, all hitting communities gouged by a decade-long recession and sharp budget cuts. In July, Tropical Storm Isaias brought yet more flooding to the island, a potent reminder of the harm that worsening climate change can wreak here.

The Center for Public Integrity and Columbia Journalism Investigations collaborated on this project with California Health Report, Centro de Periodismo Investigativo, City Limits, InvestigateWest, IowaWatch, The Island Packet, The Lens, The Mendocino Voice, Side Effects and The State.

Public Integrity's Kristine Villanueva led audience engagement for our survey of disaster survivors and mental-health professionals. She and journalists Megan Cattel, Kio Herrera, Molly Taft, and Alex Eichenstein worked on survey outreach. Rebekah Ward translated the questionnaire into Spanish. Dean Russell, Kristen Lombardi, Villanueva, and Jamie Smith Hopkins developed it, and Hopkins analyzed it.

"In the past three years, we had four major disasters," Colón Ortega said in Spanish. "In the face of all this, our emotional vulnerabilities have been heightened. ... Now, we have a collective issue of mental health that is being compounded by the lack of resources like childcare, the fear of getting infected when leaving home—we're very caring, we believe in camaraderie here, but we do have a mental-health problem."

The Center for Public Integrity, Columbia Journalism Investigations, and other newsrooms, including Centro de Periodismo Investigativo, asked people providing disaster survivors mental-health aid to share their experiences. More than two dozen from Puerto Rico responded to the questionnaire, and about 85 percent said the mental-health response they saw after Maria or other recent disasters was "poor" or "fair." Just over half described their community's overall availability and accessibility of mental-health services as "poor."

Mental-health professionals said in that survey that they are seeing more cases of anxiety and depression throughout Puerto Rico. Many said they wanted government officials to focus on establishing a disaster-readiness plan that addresses the long-term psychological needs that come after these events.

Social workers are pressing to be part of that effort. Legislation proposed in June, requested by social workers, would have recognized them as essential personnel in times of crisis. The proposal would have required employers to provide personal protective equipment to these workers and have given the profession a seat on government committees overseeing disaster response and hurricane rebuilding. But the proposal died in Puerto Rico's Senate.

Social workers say they're worried that traumatized communities will pay the price for the limitations they face doing their work during crises, such as COVID-19.

"We are now seeing situations where people are having difficulties with the isolation that comes with having to stay at home," Mabel López Ortiz, president of the College of Social Work Professionals of Puerto Rico, a regulating body of social workers in Puerto Rico, said in Spanish. "We are seeing problems of intra-family violence, domestic violence, and elderly abuse. As social workers, we are the most capable of stepping into these situations and managing these tense situations."

Two years before Maria hit, then-Gov. Alejandro Garcia Padilla said Puerto Rico was $72 billion in debt and could not repay it. Poverty measures followed, from increased taxes to cuts in social services.

The commonwealth has struggled to keep its residents from migrating to states including Florida, New York, and Texas as they search for jobs. In 2016, the president of the College of Physicians and Surgeons of Puerto Rico warned that low insurance reimbursements and increasing expenses were causing an exodus of thousands of doctors from the island.

Maria further fueled those trends: 130,000 people left Puerto Rico from July 2017 to July 2018, a period spanning the hurricane, according to the Census Bureau. Medical professionals were among that group, and they continue to leave.

"They can go to a state and charge so much more per patient," said Dr. Karen G. Martínez, director of the Center for the Study and Treatment of Fear and Anxiety at the University of Puerto Rico. "I'm the chair of the psychiatry department here … and this year, all six of our psychiatry residents, they all left for the mainland U.S."

The number of social workers on the island is also declining, according to the profession's regulating body, but it's not clear whether that's driven by moves or job cuts.

This comes as the repeated disasters undercut mental health, according to experts and residents. More than 70 survivors from Puerto Rico shared their experiences with Public Integrity, CJI and Centro de Periodismo Investigativo, and about two-thirds said they were currently or recently feeling emotional challenges they linked to a previous disaster, in most cases Maria.

Nearly as many said the coronavirus pandemic is adding to their disaster stress, anxiety, or depression.

That puts more pressure on the psychiatrists, psychologists and counselors who remain in Puerto Rico, as well as the people, including social workers, trying to provide or coordinate emotional support.

Marieli Dávila, a social worker, says she saw an immediate increase in first-time patients at the mental health clinic she was working at in Maria's aftermath.

"When we asked patients for their primary reason for coming in, we would get a variety of answers," she said in Spanish. "Some had lost their homes or their jobs, but most of them had the same starting point—Hurricane Maria."

Dávila says the federal government's systemic failures in the hurricane's aftermath worsened the mental health of survivors. In 2018, the Federal Emergency Management Agency detailed in a report how staffing shortages, logistical challenges in coordinating with local governments and a lack of supplies such as generators left the agency unprepared to adequately respond.

"There is no ... accountability when it comes to dealing with these events," Dávila said. "And we know that the government's response can't be perfect, but it can't be so vastly imperfect either."

She sees similar problems as Puerto Rico struggles to contain the spread of COVID-19. She and other social workers are coping by creating an ad hoc network of care through social media platforms, where they share information and materials to help each other give better assistance.

"We mobilized. We created a space where we could ask each other, 'Hey, what's the crisis hotline?' or 'How can I make contact with the homeless community?'" Dávila said. "The lack of designation as an essential worker doesn't keep me from doing my job, but it doesn't allow people to get the services they need. How can we come up with guidelines for visiting the elderly, for example, who are at risk of never having another visitor for the remainder of their lives, if we are not part of those committees?"

López, the president of the social worker regulating body, helped draft the proposal that would have recognized social workers as essential workers in Puerto Rico. Without that, she said, the profession is disconnected from the rest of the island's public health system during emergencies.

The governor's office declined to comment and referred questions to the Department of the Family, the agency that employs the most social workers on the island. That agency did not respond.

López had hoped the legislation to grant social workers essential worker status would become law after Sen. Miguel Romero Lugo, who represents San Juan, submitted it in June. Now, she said, it will be reworked for the next legislative session in January.

In the meantime, Lourdes Inoa Monegro, director of the women's health program for Taller Salud, a nonprofit healthcare organization, said people are trying their best. Taller Salud is based in Loiza, a largely Afro-Caribbean seaside city and one of the poorest municipalities in Puerto Rico.

After Maria, "There were people living on their rooftops. Some of these communities were underwater for two weeks. We had to deliver food and supplies to them on paddle boats," she said in Spanish. Residents went six months without electricity.

Seeing a brewing mental health crisis, Inoa Monegro gathered social workers, psychologists, and other mental-health professionals for a festival for residents that promoted joy and well-being. Workshops focused on coping and stress management. About 80 people attended and most continue to get mental-health treatment from Taller Salud today, she said.

"The government was completely ignoring the mental needs of the public because the focus is totally on the biomedical aspect of healthcare," she said. "And that's why you have social workers saying they feel neglected and the process of treating the people going through this kind of trauma is overlooked."

# CHAPTER 13

## The Puerto Rican Living Outdoors

In Guanica, P.R. residents are living precariously on the edges of roads, uncertain about a post-earthquake future.

It was the third interminable night living on the edge of a road in their wrecked Puerto Rico town, but this time the three boys huddled on an inflatable mattress had a welcome diversion. A flat-screen TV sat on milk crates that allowed them to play Mortal Kombat 11.

Hooked up to a portable generator on the bed of a pickup truck, which was parked on a grassy patch off a highway exit, the TV screen lit up as cars whizzed by just a few feet away.

"The night has arrived," Ana Ayala, 37, the mother of two of the boys, wept as she put on a sweater to fend off the evening chill. "This is the longest part."

This is the exhausting new routine for thousands of people in southern part of Puerto Rico since a magnitude-6.4 earthquake shook the island. It was after a magnitude-5.8 quake. The authorities have pleaded with them to stay with relatives or at least congregate at outdoor camps receiving food and medical aid.

Families like Ms. Ayala's, afraid to go home to buildings that could collapse in future quakes, have insisted on setting up camp in other public spaces. They were posing a new challenge for strained government services and aid workers. Streets lined with homes look like ghost towns, while parking lots are packed with tailgate chairs, tents, and cots.

Rafael Rodríguez Mercado, the Puerto Rico health secretary, urged the evacuees roughing it on their own to move to the government-run camps for their safety and to avoid an outbreak of gastrointestinal disease.

This is the exhausting new routine for thousands of people in southern Puerto Rico since a magnitude-6.4 earthquake shook the island on Tuesday, a day after a magnitude-5.8 quake. The authorities have pleaded with them to stay with relatives or at least congregate at outdoor camps receiving food and medical aid.

It is not that Ms. Ayala and the five other families camped there. All are relatives, friends, or neighbors. They do not want the assistance provided at a government-run shelter.

José Luis Casiano, Ms. Ayala's husband wanted to be on higher ground and closer to the highway leading out of town in the event of a tsunami, perhaps the biggest fear among residents following more than a week of unsettling tremors. Mr. Casiano and the others first ventured to the grassy patch on Dec. 28, though at first, they spent the night in their cars.

After Tuesday's big shake, which briefly triggered a tsunami watch and set local sirens blaring, the families deployed in earnest, parking a half-dozen S.U.V.s in a protective semicircle around their blue tent.

I haven't seen a bed since Three Kings Day," said José David Quiñones Nazario, 40, as he sat on a patio chair, mosquito zapper in hand as the insects swarmed at dusk.

Two chairs down, Fenixa Muñoz quietly rocked her sleeping 6-month-old son, Matthew. His playpen was a few feet away. The quake leveled the bakery Ms. Muñoz and her husband, Germaine Vélez, 34, opened nearly three years ago. Fourteen employees were left jobless. Their 10-year-old son, Sebastián, has not wanted to eat or sleep or speak much since the temblor.

The bakery's big generator is now set up in the camp, used at night to turn on one of three spotlights.

"Guánica is destroyed," lamented Mayra Rivera, 38, Mr. Quiñones's wife.

The quake knocked over everything inside her house, she said. She must sign up for a structural engineering inspection but has not done so yet. It is all too overwhelming.

"I've been showering in the patio of my house," said Gladys Rodríguez, 68, Ms. Rivera's mother. "I won't go inside."

Ms. Ayala's 10-year-old son, Yonatan Elí García, wearing red swimming trunks, improvised a shower on Wednesday afternoon by standing behind an open S.U.V. door while his grandmother held a modesty towel on the other side and his grandfather poured a gallon of water over his head.

The evening coffee came out of a Mr. Coffee pot balanced on a crate and plugged into the portable generator.

A towel and jeans air-dried on tree branches. Between two sets of trees, Mr. Casiano, 37, strung a pair of striped hammocks. From the tent hung a stalk of green bananas.

Complicating the return home, about half of the island, 850,000 customers, remained without power on Thursday. José Ortiz, the director of the Puerto Rico Electric Power Authority, said the public utility hoped to fully restore electricity by Sunday, but his rosier estimates earlier in the week have proved wrong. Gov. Wanda Vázquez was more cautious. "We can't speak of exact dates," she said. "No one can say that."

Transportation officials closed a portion of the main highway from San Juan, the capital, to the damaged southern town of Ponce, citing serious structural damage to the roof of a tolling plaza near Ponce.

Federal Emergency Management Agency officials sat down with local mayors on Thursday to assess their needs. One mayor, Angel Luis Torres of Yauco, said he walked out of the meeting in Ponce frustrated by the onerous bureaucracy in his attempts to get water, generators, and tents to the nearly 3,000 people in his town who are sleeping outside.

He fears that people will refuse to return home until engineers inspect their homes. With some 300 houses damaged by the quake in his town alone, inspectors are scarce.

"How are we going to tell people to go back home?" Mr. Torres asked.

At the roadside camp in Guánica, municipal workers have come by every day to fill a huge potable water container, which Ms. Ayala and her friends and neighbors use to rinse silverware and wash up.

On Wednesday night, the Rev. Luis Vidal Ortiz from the Iglesia de Dios Pentecostal pulled up in a small yellow school bus and delivered packs of chips, cookies, and personal hygiene products.

He invited the families to visit the church for a hot meal on Friday. Later, a convoy of flatbed trucks, led by the mayor and other public officials, came by with water bottles. A crew installed a portable floodlight across the street for safety.

At the nearby sports complex where the government is running a local camp, evacuees had access to indoor bathrooms. Although without running water, as well as to a mobile clinic, a dinner of arroz con pollo, volunteer physicians and a group of psychologists offering art therapy and crisis counseling.

The families at the roadside encampment acknowledged that they felt, indeed, in the middle of a crisis. Mr. Casiano's eyes welled with tears remembering the big quake on Tuesday. His German shepherd, Zukari, had been acting strangely right before, breathing hard and raising her head in alert, he said. Since then, "we've felt the earth shake even when it's not shaking," Mr. Casiano said. "At night, we shiver twice: from the shaking and from the cold."

"We're staying until the power comes back on, and the water," he added. "Or if the police evacuate the town."

Moments later, Zukari, who was leashed to a tree, barked. The ground quivered.

Ms. Ayala called out a warning of a new aftershock: "¡Tembló!"

# CHAPTER 14

# Earthquakes Trigger Anxiety in Puerto Rico

After the worst earthquake in more than a century killed one person and triggered an island wide blackout in Puerto Rico, many people couldn't find the strength to go back into their homes.

"It was very shocking. Our mirrors, our drawers, our paintings fell out," Nazario, 47, a high school math teacher and a community activist, said. "People are sad, worried and many are inconsolable. My family is very nervous, and my wife is very affected, she doesn't even want to be inside our house."

As if the 6.4-magnitude quake on Tuesday that destroyed schools, churches and homes wasn't enough, it has been followed by more than 80 aftershocks. The biggest aftershock happened on Saturday morning.

At about 9 a.m. local time, a 5.9-magnitude shock caused more damage, mainly in areas around the southern coast where hundreds of homes and schools had already collapsed from Tuesday's temblor.

The series of earthquakes come two years after Hurricane Maria hit in September 2017, the worst natural disaster in the island's modern history.

Nazario said that after the hurricane and now the temblors, "some people feel like the earthquake is some sort of divine punishment."

He tries to help by reminding people that such events are just the way nature works.

Christine Nieves co-founded a cooperative open-air kitchen and neighborhood resource center, Proyecto de Apoyo Mutuo Mariana, after Maria hit. She did it mainly so that people, especially those living alone, would have somewhere to go when they were scared and living in darkness.

Maria caused the world's second-longest blackout, which lasted over a year.

After the earthquake, there was a lot of anxiety because "we feel like we're back to the post-Maria times," said Nieves, who lives in Humacao.

"Asking people to remain calm is not easy when they have <u>PTSD</u>," she said, referring to <u>post-traumatic stress disorder</u>. "We really need to work on our collective psychology, our collective mental health."

Puerto Ricans have not lived through a devastating earthquake in more than 100 years. The memories of the post-Maria scenario are still very fresh, with an island wide power outage and hundreds of thousands who lost water access because electrical water pumps weren't working.

Many who fear that their homes could crumble and collapse overnight if another earthquake hit moved their beds outdoors. They sleep outside every night until dawn.

People on the island are still experiencing <u>PTSD</u> more than two years after Maria, which killed at least 2,975 people, according to the American Psychological Association.

A survey conducted one year after the hurricane revealed that over one-fifth of the island's residents reported needing or receiving mental health services. Thirteen percent said they started a new or a higher dose of prescription medications to treat emotional problems.

More than seven percent of all children in Puerto Rico meet clinical standards for <u>PTSD</u>, a rate twice than that of the general population.

The 6.4-magnitude earthquake awoke many unwanted memories of Maria among Puerto Ricans from all walks of life, from families and children to public officials, and the persistent aftershocks continue to rattle the residents.

San Juan Mayor Carmen Yulín Cruz told NBC News there's fear and even panic at the thought of fighting with the uncertainty of another life-threatening situation.

"Those are painful memories, memories that you not only have in your head but that scar on your soul," Cruz said.

She and other leaders face the mental and physical challenge of ensuring "we don't transmit to our people an attitude of defeat, or of nothing can be done."

"You can't go home because it may fall on you, so your life is changed in an instant. Your memories are in your home, your food, your clothing. Everything is shattered and you woke up to a different reality," she said.

Gov. Wanda Vázquez announced that she has declared a major state emergency after an initial assessment following the latest temblor.

The quakes have caused $110 million in damage and have destroyed at least 559 structures island wide, she said.

After earthquakes, Guánica's main street and buildings saw severe damage. Part of the city hall collapsed, as well as the main hardware store. Small businesses in neighborhoods such as Barrio La Luna also crumbled.

Nazario said that that quake separated his neighbor's carport from the house and destroyed their kitchen. Dramatic landslides in his neighborhood of Bosque Seco blocked the street where he resides.

He started fielding calls from anxious parents saying they didn't want to send their children to school. He was worried about children dropping out, especially those whose schools were permanently closed after Maria and who face grueling, long commutes to schools in farther towns.

When schools were reopened after Maria, Nazario said being there felt like a "therapy session." When schools open, he thinks it may be the same.

"We give them our support and let them know that this is a natural disaster, and we'll try to help them," he said.

Hundreds of small earthquakes have been shaking Puerto Rico since Dec. 28, prompting an increase in calls to a government-run mental health hotline known as Línea PAS, according to Suzanne Roig, the main administrator of Puerto Rico's Office of Mental Health Services and Addiction Prevention.

Aside from the hotline, Nieves said the government could do more to help "provide clear guidance and mechanism to work within communities" in need of mental health services.

Puerto Rico is slowly recovering from the latest disaster. Most customers had their electricity and water supply restored.

The conversation happening in almost every household "is about how to stay safe during an earthquake."

Nieves said, "our trauma makes us prepare for a hurricane," but a hurricane and an earthquake are not the same, and she's worried about the lack of knowledge surrounding earthquake preparedness.

"There's a lot of talk about the emergency backpack," Nieves said, referring to a bag full of essentials that most Puerto Ricans now have following Maria for use in case they must quickly leave their homes.

Unlike hurricanes, earthquakes can hit with no warning. Despite the anxiety over the unknown, "it's crucial to know where the nearest nurses are, where the elderly people live, where are our resources. That saves more lives than the backpack."

# CHAPTER 15

# Puerto Ricans Fled to Florida

Jose Santiago was worried about his two adult daughters as Hurricane Dorian threatened Puerto Rico.

When the island dodged a direct hit from the storm, his daughters became increasingly concerned about the direction of the hurricane. This storm was going straight for Florida where Santiago had moved after Hurricane Maria ravaged the island in September 2017.

"One of them told me, 'Daddy, this isn't going to hit Puerto Rico directly, but now I'm worried about you,'" said Santiago, who drives cars for an auction house in Orlando.

Like Santiago, tens of thousands of Puerto Ricans moved to Florida after Hurricane Maria to escape the devastation of the Category 4 storm. Now, they're facing a potentially destructive storm in the very place where they sought refuge.

Living through Hurricane Maria taught Santiago the importance of preparing for a storm, and he has purchased a generator, canned food, and water. He's betting Dorian won't be as bad.

"Maria was like almost 200 miles per hour, 322 kph. It was scary with the noise and stuff, and the wind," said Santiago, who exaggerated a bit—maximum sustained winds were 155 mph, 249 kph, by the time the storm reached Puerto Rico. "I don't think Dorian is going to be a third of what Maria was."

Hurricane Maria was a Category 4 storm by the time it hit Puerto Rico, leaving a death toll of around 3,000. Many Puerto Ricans who had been recovering from Hurricane Irma two weeks earlier, were left with a power grid that was essentially destroyed and a lack of tap water and cellphone service.

What had been a steady flow of residents leaving the island because of economic hardship became a flow after the storm. The U.S. Census Bureau estimates around 130,000 Puerto Ricans moved away between July 2017 and July 2018.

The Bureau of Economic and Business Research at the University of Florida estimated that as many as 50,000 of them settled in Florida after Hurricane Maria.

Florida now has more than 1.1 million Puerto Ricans and has exceeded New York as the state with the largest number of Puerto Ricans living on the mainland.

During Hurricane Dorian's polish with Puerto Rico. Idalis Fernandez worried about her cousins and aunts on the island, who lost power, but they were otherwise fine. Like Santiago's daughters, they were more concerned about her living in Florida.

"They've already called me twice, asking me, 'What are you going to do?'" said Fernandez, who moved to Orlando after Hurricane Maria and now works as a server.

Fernandez had already purchased her food supplies and packed everything into the fridge. She had removed chairs from the porch of her apartment and secured other items.

Her 12-year-old son, Alexander, was worried they would be without power for months, like they were in Puerto Rico after Hurricane Maria

"I tell him he needs to be calm because I'm here and we have everything here," Fernandez said. "I tell him, 'Just wait and pray.'"

# CHAPTER 16

# After Maria

Two and half weeks after Hurricane Maria hammered Puerto Rico, Ivan Nieves's grandfather had few options. He was not able to get chemotherapy for his prostate cancer, and his main doctor had left the island.

So, Nieves, 29, made a quick decision, and on Oct. 8, he boarded a plane for Miami with his grandparents, his mother, and his partner.

The same day the hurricane hit, Nieves was supposed to sign a contract to open a second location for his bistro, juice bar and organic bakery. Instead, six months later, he and his partner are completing renovations in a space in the historic MiMo district of Miami for La Social, which will offer the same menu as his business in San Juan.

"I'm staying because I'm looking to grow," Nieves said. "In Puerto Rico, we went backward after the hurricane."

It is a refrain that has been repeated in recent months by tens of thousands of Puerto Ricans who have closed shops, quit jobs, and raced to Florida, transforming cities across the state.

It's the largest migration ever from the Caribbean Island, already surpassing the one after World War II.

To come up with the figure, Rayer looked at the number of people who arrived at airports in Miami and Orlando. There was a total that includes government workers, volunteers, journalists, and people making multiple trips.

He then compared that figure to the number of Puerto Ricans who used the disaster relief centers set up by the state and the number of children who have enrolled in kindergarten through 12th grade in public schools.

Over 135,000 Puerto Ricans have relocated to the U.S. mainland since the hurricane, according to a report released by the Center for Puerto Rican Studies at Hunter College in New York. The majority have gone to Florida.

Stefan Rayer, the population program director at the University of Florida's Bureau of Economic and Business Research, estimates that roughly 50,000 to 75,000 Puerto Ricans may have permanently settled in Florida since the storm.

It appears the invasion will continue. Jorge Duany, the director of the Cuban Research Institute at Florida International University and an expert in Puerto Rican migration, conducted a randomized telephone poll with 351 island residents in January.

Every person he spoke to said they were thinking of moving to the mainland, and over 65 percent were planning to permanently relocate.

Puerto Ricans have a long history in Florida. By the late 1800s, they were settling in the Tampa Bay area and later in South Florida.

"Historically, Miami-Dade County had a much larger Puerto Rican population before Central Florida," Duany said.

It wasn't until the 1980s that Puerto Ricans started moving in significant numbers to Orlando and other parts of Central Florida. These included islanders as well as Puerto Ricans from New York and Chicago.

It was Puerto Rico's economic crisis, which began in 2006, that provoked a massive wave. The Puerto Rican population in Florida has shot up to over 1 million, from 479,000 in 2000, according to the Pew Research Center.

After Hurricane Maria left damages of over $94 billion, the pace of Puerto Rican arrivals increased dramatically. Many were already thinking of leaving, but the storm's aftermath precipitated the move.

Rafael Ortiz Perez, 57, a civil engineer from Salinas in the southern part of Puerto Rico, arrived in Miami on Oct. 28, after the hurricane's fierce winds blew the roof off his house.

"The move has been positive," Ortiz-Perez said. "Things in Puerto Rico have not been good. Maria helped me make the final decision to move."

Initially, he stayed with his mother, who had settled in Miami 35 years ago. Shortly after arriving, he was hired by a Puerto Rican-owned architectural firm and is now working on a project with NASA.

Luis DeRosa, president of the Puerto Rican Chamber of Commerce of South Florida, said he is seeing more well-educated islanders moving to the area.

He has been helping countless Puerto Rican businesspeople establish their operations in South Florida.

"The Puerto Ricans coming to open businesses are here to stay," De Rosa said. "They've done their homework."

With so many arriving, the impact is being felt in schools, politics, and housing.

Over 11,700 Puerto Rican children have registered in Florida's public schools. In Miami-Dade County, new students have enrolled in numerous schools across the county, so it has not caused a strain in any one school.

The county has hired 65 Puerto Rican instructional employees who were displaced after the hurricane. Orange County, in Central Florida, has 89 new hires from the island.

As U.S. citizens, Puerto Ricans are eligible to vote once they move here and register. They have the potential to influence elections in one of the country's most crucial swing states.

Gov. Rick Scott, a Republican and likely U.S. Senate candidate, declared a state of emergency in early October to help the state provide services and obtain federal money to help Puerto Ricans displaced by the hurricane. He also established disaster relief centers to provide newcomers with information about schools, medical care, and jobs.

Across 41 states and Puerto Rico, over 3,500 families are staying in hotels under the Federal Emergency Management Agency's Transitional Shelter Assistance program. More than 1,300 of them are in Florida.

Colleges and universities in Florida have offered in-state tuition to students from Puerto Rico; Florida International University has 216 such students currently enrolled.

Most of the stays end on March 20. Jackeline Soto Perez, 29, a nurse, is nervously counting the days until the deadline. She, her husband and two children, 3 and 7, have been able to stay in a Miami hotel through the program. They have found an apartment to rent, but it's not available until April 1, so they are figuring out where to stay in the meantime.

In her hometown, Añasco, in western Puerto Rico, the lack of electricity after the hurricane was becoming untenable. Perez's younger son has neutropenia, a condition that reduces the body's ability to fight bacterial infections. His daily medication needs refrigeration, a daunting task without electricity. It's what ultimately led them to flee the island.

On a recent afternoon, she touched his forehead, checking for fever, as he slept. Perez was worried because he had not been feeling well.

Perez's husband is a paramedic, and she is a home health aide, working an overnight shift three times a week in West Palm Beach, often facing a two-and-half-hour drive to work.

Despite the challenges, the family has no plans to return. "My parents are in Puerto Rico, so it's rough," she said. "But as long as I have a good job here, I wouldn't leave."

# CHAPTER 17

# Fleeing to Florida after Hurricane Maria

Tens of thousands of Puerto Rico residents are fleeing to Florida after Hurricane Maria, leaving behind an island that is still struggling to regain power more than one month after the storm.

About 70% of the US territory, which is home to approximately 3.4 million US citizens, is still without power. Many do not have access to reliable drinking water.

"Since October 3, 2017, more than 73,000 individuals arrived in Florida from Puerto Rico through Miami International Airport, Orlando International Airport and the Everglades Port," Florida Gov. Rick Scott's office said in a statement.

The United States approved Florida to host residents with the help of the Federal Emergency Management Agency on October 5, he said.

"This agreement approves 100% federal reimbursement for costs incurred by the state of Florida related to the accommodation of those displaced by Hurricane Maria," he said.

The state has opened three disaster relief centers at the main airports in Orlando, Miami, and the Port of Miami for displaced families from Puerto Rico.

Staff from several agencies, including FEMA and the American Red Cross, are in Florida helping incoming residents, he said.

Those heading to the US mainland are leaving behind an island that's almost in total darkness. Puerto Rico and the U.S. Virgin Islands are during the largest blackout in US history, according to a report from an economic research company.

In all, Hurricane Maria has caused a loss of 1.25 billion hours of electricity supply for Americans, according to the analysis from the Rhodium Group. That makes it the largest blackout in US history, well ahead of Hurricane Georges in 1998 and Superstorm Sandy in 2012, the group said.

That 1.25 billion number will continue to grow. More than a month after Hurricane Maria knocked out the electric grid on the islands, most residents remain without electricity, and the restoration of that power is months away.

Getting power back to hilltop communities like Aguas Buenas after Hurricane Maria requires work in tough terrain.

As of Thursday, just 26% of households had power restored, according to the Puerto Rico Electric Power Authority.

The state-owned utility filed for bankruptcy in July, is $9 billion in debt and is struggling to recover from the hurricane outages. Not coincidentally, several of the top 10 blackouts in US history involve Puerto Rico, including Maria and Irma this year and Hurricane Georges in 1998.

Whitefish Energy, a two-year-old utility firm with ties to the Trump administration, was awarded a $300 million contract to help restore the country's power grid. The huge contract to a small company has drawn questions and criticism.

# CHAPTER 18

◇◇◇◇◇◇◇

# Hurricane Maria Survivors

Unlike many of their neighbors, Sasha Justiniano and her mother, Noemi Ortiz, remained wary after Hurricane Irma skirted Puerto Rico Sept. 6, 2017. They knew others could follow.

But even they weren't ready for the humanitarian crisis Hurricane Maria brought ashore 14 days later with its 175 mph winds, rain, and storm surge.

Left behind after the storm passed were 2,975 dead, destroyed homes and businesses, downed power lines, and other catastrophic damage—further battering the struggling economy of Puerto Rico.

Ortiz, a community service officer who helped the Puerto Rican government meet residents' housing, food, and other needs, thought she had done everything to ready herself for the approaching storm.

"We prepared, and went to the store, and got about two weeks' worth of food and water," she said. "But once Hurricane Maria hit, we realized it wasn't going to be enough."

Major bridges and roadways were gone, she said, cutting them off. "There was no way in or out," Ortiz said. "We were stuck. Neighbors tried to help each other clear the roads, but we didn't have any heavy equipment."

Panicked residents fought for water and waited hours for dwindling supplies of gasoline. The tire shop where Justiniano worked took days to reach, and when she finally got there, she learned that the business couldn't operate until electricity was restored.

Justiniano and Ortiz remain shaken to this day when they talk about Hurricane Maria's fury.

"Most people weren't doing anything to prepare, because they said Maria wasn't coming either, just like Irma," Justiniano said. "When the storm hit, we could hear people screaming and running outside, and houses exploding, and trees falling, and leaves and debris hitting the house. Our house was made of concrete, and we were safer, but we had left the windows open since we thought our house may explode or implode."

"We could feel the wind in our ears," Ortiz said. "It sounded like a monster outside."

A birthday present Ortiz gave Justiniano before the storm hit. It was a Caribbean cruise and plane tickets for both to the port near Orlando. This provided their escape to Florida in November 2017.

They left with a single suitcase each, and except for one trip back for items left behind, they have remained in Florida ever since.

While living with Ortiz's sister in Clermont, Justiniano applied for a bilingual teller position at a local Wells Fargo bank branch.

"When I asked her to tell me a little about herself and her work experience at the tire shop in Puerto Rico, her lower lip started to twinge a bit, and then she told me her story," Ashley Hebert, the Wells Fargo branch service manager who interviewed her, said. "A week before that I had been in Houston, Texas, helping my own dad recover after his house and truck were flooded by Hurricane Harvey. Her story went straight to my heart."

Justiniano joined Hebert's team on March 19, 2018, and not long after, she and Ortiz moved into their own apartment.

"It was a big adjustment for us both moving here, emotionally and financially, but we have accomplished a lot," said Ortiz, who takes English courses online at night.

By day, she works at a local hospital sterilizing medical equipment. "These are challenges we need to overcome, and that we will overcome.

"When we first moved here, Sasha would cry every single day," Ortiz said. "The biggest change has been the job at Wells Fargo because it has opened opportunities for her and been a huge shift in her life and helped change her perspective.

"As a mom, I am proud of what she's been able to accomplish, and the way she feels for and cares about others.

Jaimie Urbaez and Yasel Fleitas also survived Hurricane Maria's destruction in Puerto Rico, and they too found their way to Wells Fargo in the storm's aftermath.

Before becoming a teller at a Wells Fargo branch in Orlando, Florida, in February 2018, Urbaez worked as service manager for a bank near San Juan. With two small children, a 5-year-old daughter and 2-year-old son, Urbaez said worsening conditions in Puerto Rico prompted her and her mother, Zulma, to flee to Orlando, where her brother lives.

"I felt super comfortable joining Wells Fargo because it was an industry I already knew," Urbaez said. "I felt good, and Wells Fargo made it super easy for me to adapt.

"After Maria, conditions were horrible, and everything was difficult," she said. "I didn't have a generator, so it was hard for me to have my children in a place without air conditioning, electricity, and fresh food, and to go to work and leave them with my mom in those conditions. I couldn't leave my kids like that."

Fleitas also had prior banking experience. He had already worked for Wells Fargo for eight years in a variety of roles at bank branches in Miami when he and his partner headed to Puerto Rico in January 2018 to run La Social, a hair salon, bistro, and boutique in San Juan.

The business emerged from Irma unscathed, but not Maria. Floodwaters swamped the neighborhood, and so many customers left as they struggled to recover from the storm themselves that Fleitas couldn't keep it open.

"It was sad to see such a beautiful island destroyed," said Fleitas. "Nothing was green, but gray. The ocean was no longer blue, but black. I knew it was going to be hard to recover. Friends and customers that I met along the way started coming to the mainland.

Took ownership of my destiny and made the decision to leave all dreams and ambitions behind once again," he said. "I packed what I could and left on the first flight to Miami. Not knowing where and how to start was the most horrifying feeling. After all I once had, the question on my mind was: Will I be successful again?"

He soon got his answer when his prior Wells Fargo boss called about a job while he was living with his parents in Miami. He rejoined the company March 15, 2018. "I'll forever be grateful and thankful to Wells Fargo for the opportunity to re-establish myself and my reputation with so much love and support.

It helped me get back on my feet and recuperate from having left behind a dream crashed by nature.

According to The City University of New York's Center for Puerto Rican Studies, Justiniano, Urbaez, and Fleitas are among more than 300,000 Puerto Ricans estimated to have left the island after Hurricane Maria.

A population shift has been underway for more than a decade, the center said that 525,769 Puerto Ricans have moved to the continental U.S. from 2006 to 2016. The storm accelerated this shift.

The center, which is leading efforts to rebuild Puerto Rico, estimates another 470,000 residents could leave between 2017 and 2019 because of Hurricane Maria.

While 49 of 50 states have received residents after the storm, Florida has received the most, nearly 42 percent of all in-migration from Puerto Rico. Within Florida, the Orlando area has attracted the most transplants.

Gaby Ortigoni, president of the Hispanic Chamber of Commerce of Metro Orlando, said family connections, welcoming communities, multiple direct flights from Orlando International Airport, and a fast-growing Hispanic population led thousands of Puerto Ricans.

Ortigoni said the chamber, Prospera, an economic development nonprofit that helps Hispanic entrepreneurs open or expand businesses and companies like Wells Fargo are helping small business owners from Puerto Rico both expand into Florida while strengthening their operations on the island.

From October 2017 to June 2018, Prospera has assisted at least 500 Puerto Rican business owners who have expressed an interest in expanding to Central Florida, Ortigoni said.

Puerto Ricans have comprised more than half of Prospera's business development seminars attendees, added Ortigoni, and 40 percent of Prospera's consulting clients in the region have been Puerto Ricans.

"The estimated number of people who have moved from Puerto Rico to stay in Central Florida fluctuates between 50,000 to more than 300,000," said Ortigoni

In addition to supporting small-business development, Wells Fargo worked with the Red Cross to drop-ship care packages to Puerto Rico after Hurricane Maria and contributed $575,000 for disaster relief in Puerto Rico, Mexico, and Asia following disasters. Wells Fargo Consumer Banking team members in El Paso, Texas, added to those efforts by sending new toys, board games, puzzles, and art supplies to the Puerto Rico Soccer League for children during the holidays.

"As we have had folks migrate from Puerto Rico and seek to re-establish themselves here, we've worked with organizations like the Hispanic Chamber of Commerce and Prospera to aid these thousands of customers in that transition," said Derek Jones, Central Florida region bank president for Wells Fargo. "We know one of the keyways to do that is to establish yourself financially, and having Sasha and others like her has helped us be there for our customers."

Jones said Justiniano's story continues to inspire him, just as it has inspired her team members and customers.

"We really believe in hiring a diverse population to mirror our community, and also believe strongly in developing our team members so they can provide the best experience for our customers," Jones said. "Sasha's story is a perfect example of how both played out here in Central Florida."

Hebert still marvels at how Justiniano moved from a majority Spanish-speaking territory to one where English is the predominant language, and how she taught herself English.

"We call Sasha our little warrior," Hebert said. "She inspires us every day because of what we all know she's been through, even though you'd never guess it from her attitude. She's always smiling. Still, to this day she says, 'Ashley, thank you for this opportunity. Thank you for bringing me aboard. Thank you for giving me a chance to start over.' She is so humble and grateful.

Her strength has made all of us strong as a team. We've always been a really strong team, but she has brought our close-knit family together even more and made us that much stronger. She is amazing and left us all wanting to be even better for our customers and each other."

Justiniano feels the same way about Hebert and her team members.

"Thank God Wells Fargo gave me the opportunity," she said. "Like my mom always says, I know that "If you work hard and stay positive, you can get through anything.'"

# CHAPTER 19

# Massive Exodus To The Main Land

The massive exodus of Puerto Ricans heading to the mainland started in 2006 with the island's recession. Then came the government's debt crisis of 2014 and more people left.

After hurricanes Maria and Irma, people also left to the point that the Pew Research Center released a study in 2018 said that the island's population had reached a 40-year low.

Now, the recent earthquakes that started in December of 2019 and have continued through the first weeks of 2020 are giving Puerto Ricans another reason to leave.

Many went to Texas…

So, who is left in Puerto Rico now that the middle class has left?

One group is formed of people who literally can't move: people who are too sick, too frail, or too old to leave.

"In 2018 about 1 in 5 people in Puerto Rico were 65 years or older," says Jens Manuel Krogstad, an expert in population with the Pew Research Center. He says that while other groups in the island shrunk over the last decade, the number of elderly people there is on the rise.

Of course, the government class is staying, and people who love their land also refuse to leave. People with means and people in industry are staying, too. The tourism industry is one that is still relatively strong.

More than 3 million people visited Puerto Rico in 2018. That is telling us that there are two reasons….

One is that happened right after the hurricanes; the other reason is that there were about the same number of people visiting the island as the number who permanently live there.

The Coffee Spot is a café near a U.S. military beach in Aguadilla on the northwestern tip of Puerto Rico. Willie Florenciani is the owner. He says a lot of families with children are leaving. Speaking in his native Spanish, he says "many worry about how sound school buildings are after the earthquakes."

They have reasons to worry because one elementary school is among the buildings that recently collapsed.

Although his heart breaks every time a local stop by for their last cappuccino on the island, Florenciani understands why they are leaving. After all, he is a father, too. He is staying put, for several reasons: for one thing, his family is financially stable; he also employs 20 people.

"So, it's not just about me," Florenciani says, over the phone. "These families depend on me."

In the aftermath of Hurricane Maria, lots of Puerto Ricans are setting their sights on becoming Texans...

Since Puerto Rico is a territory of the U.S., its citizens are American citizens, too. They are free to re locate anywhere in the 50 states.

Mildred Lopez, a Puerto Rican community organizer, and wife of the pastor of the Emanuel Church in Plano, says the members of her church are all Puerto Rican. Many, including Lopez' husband, have family on the island who are hoping to move to Texas. Some temporarily, many for the long haul.

Her husband and his brothers are planning to bring their parents to Texas for at least a couple of months.

"They are elderly. They don't have the food; they don't have the water. It's very difficult for them," Lopez says.

Lopez says her church is preparing to welcome other families that are leaving the island. Texas is an attractive destination for Puerto Ricans at any time, Lopez says.

"There's a lot of jobs here in Texas," she says. "The education is great. I think that by word of mouth, people are going to start moving to Texas..."

Despite the devastation in Puerto Rico, Lopez thinks the people will rebuild.

"I know that my island is going to rise," she says. "I know that my island is going to be restored. I know that my island is going to rebuild. But it's going to take time."

# CHAPTER 20

# 2019–2020 Puerto Rico's Earthquakes

Start it out on December 28, 2019, and advancing into 2020, the southwestern part of the island of Puerto Rico was struck by an earthquake mass, including 11 that were of magnitude 5 or greater.

The largest and most damaging of this sequence was a magnitude 6.4 Mw, which occurred on January 7 at 04:24 AST, 08:24 UTC, with a maximum felt intensity of VIII, Severe, on the Modified Mercalli intensity scale.

At least one person was killed, and several others were injured.

A 5.8 Mw earthquake the previous day caused the destruction of a natural arch, a tourist attraction at Punta Ventana in Guayanilla.

A 5.9 Mw aftershock on Saturday, January 11, 2020, damaged many structures, including several historical buildings as well as modern high-rises in the city of Ponce, my hometown.

Power was lost island-wide immediately after the quake and was increasingly restored over a period of a week. Damage to homes was extensive and, by January 14, 2020, more than 8,000 people were homeless and camping outdoors in various types of shelters, with 40,000 others camping outside their homes, just in the city of Ponce alone.

There were refugees in 28 government-sponsored refugee centers spread over 14 municipalities of southern and central Puerto Rico. Damage to government structures was calculated in the hundreds of millions and financial losses were estimated in $3.1 billion.

A power plant that supplied over a quarter of Puerto Rico's energy needs was badly damaged and was shut down, with repairs estimated to take at least a year.

The day of the main quake, January 7, 2020, Puerto Rico Governor Wanda Vázquez Garced declared a state of emergency and activated the Puerto Rico National Guard and the Puerto Rico State Guard. That same day, she also made available $130 million in aid to the municipalities affected.

The White House also approved $5 million in federal emergency relief....

On January 12, 2020, the day after the January 11. 2020, 5.9 aftershock, the governor distributed $12 million to six municipalities most affected by the quake. Tent cities were set up in five of the hardest-hit towns with space for some 3,200 refugees.

Puerto Rico lies at the highly oblique convergent boundary between the Caribbean Plate and the North American Plate. A separate Puerto Rico–Virgin Islands microplate has been identified based on GPS observations.

To the north in the North American Plate is being subducted beneath this microplate along the Puerto Rico Trench. To the south of Puerto Rico, the microplate is being thrust southwards over the Caribbean Plate along the Muertos Thrust system.

On the upper slope and shelf the current style of faulting is extensional with a series of WSW-ENE trending normal faults, such as the Ponce Fault and the Bajo Tasmanian Fault. Several faults are also known to cross parts of the main island.

The sequence began on December 28, 2019, with a Mw 4.7 earthquake, followed closely by a Mw 5.0 event in the early hours of December 29. 2019 Several earthquakes of M <5 occurred over the next few days, followed by a Mw 5.8 event at 10:32 UTC on January 6. 2020.

The largest event, a Mw 6.4, occurred the next morning, followed by a Mw 5.6 event within 10 minutes and a Mw 5.0 about 15 minutes after that. The Mw 6.4 event had a focal mechanism consistent with normal faulting on a fault trending WSW-ENE.

A Mw 5.9 event was then logged on January 11, 2020, at 12:54 UTC. In the first month of the sequence there were a total of 11 M ≥5 earthquakes and a further 82 in the range M 4–4.9. A Mw 5.4 earthquake occurred on May 2 at 11:13 UTC in the same area as the M 6.4 event and with a similar focal mechanism.

As of May 2, 2020, after a further two M>4 shocks in the same area, the total number of earthquakes in the sequence of M>3 exceeded 1,000 and there had been 95 of M>4.

Puerto Rico governor Wanda Vázquez Garced declared a state of emergency on January 7, 2020, and mobilized the Puerto Rico National Guard.

On January 8, the day after the main quake, the Ponce municipal government registered 1,111 residents in city shelters, "not including hundreds more" who drove to government-designated meeting sites, such as Estadio Paquito Montaner, to sleep in their cars.

The parking lot at Auditorio Juan Pachin Vicens was also used as a meeting site.

The Bernardino Cordero Bernard Vocational High School was also used as a shelter.

The night after the quake, it was estimated that over 40,000 Ponce residents chose to sleep in their cars instead of their homes out of fear of more quakes.

By January 13, 2020, the number of refugees was estimated at around 3,000 Island-wide, but the municipal officials of some local governments believed that figure was probably about right for refugees in just their own single municipalities.

Another estimates out the number of refugees at 5,000…

On January 7, 2020, the Puerto Rican government made available $130 million in aid. Late January 7, FEMA confirmed that US president Donald Trump had issued a non-disaster, emergency declaration with a $5 million cap.

The $5 million emergency declaration monies were to be spent on emergency services only.

On January 12, 2020, Puerto Rico governor Wanda Vázquez Garced made a disbursement of $2 million to each of six municipalities most affected by the quake; the monies came from the Puerto Rico State Emergency Reserve Fund.

The government set up a central command center, where all pertinent state and municipal dependencies supporting the relief effort were to set up base and coordinate activities at the Polydeportivo Frankie Colon in Urbanización Los Caobos, Barrio Bucaná, Ponce. It also became a collection center for items for the earthquake homeless.

By January 14, 2020, over 600 soldiers of the Puerto Rico National Guard had set up five tent cities for the homeless, with at least some tents outfitted with air conditioning for the bed-ridden and the elderly, in the towns of Guánica, Yauco, Guayanilla, Peñuelas and Ponce, with facilities for over 3,200 refugees.

A man died in Urbanization Jardines del Caribe in the city of Ponce as a direct result of the January 7, 2020, quake, and eight others were injured also in Ponce.

A woman died of a heart attack in the town of Guayanilla after a 4.36-magnitude aftershock hit overnight during the night of January 9 to January 10, 2020.

By January 10, 2020, two additional people had died of medical conditions attributed to the effects of the earthquakes.

There were refugees in 28 government-sponsored refugee centers in the southern and central Puerto Rico municipalities of Yauco, Guánica, Ponce, Peñuelas, Guayanilla, Utuado, Maricao, Juana Díaz, Adjuntas, Sabana Grande, San Germán, Lajas, Jayuya and Mayagüez.

The quakes also caused 28 families in Lares to lose their homes.

At least three residential high-rise buildings in Ponce were rendered unusable, leaving the residents homeless.

On January 13, 2020, it was reported that some 3,000 homes had been destroyed or significantly damaged.

By January 14, 2020, the number of homeless region-wide had climbed to 8,000.

On January 15, 2020, it was register at least 789 properties that were damaged.

The number of homes with some level of damage was, however, significantly higher. For example, according to its mayor, in the town of Yauco alone, there were 3,200 homes with some degree of damage.

Numerous authorities pointed to the emotional toll on the people, particularly on entire families who had been left homeless.

The January 7, 2020, quake destroyed numerous structures, including the Agripina Seda elementary school in Guánica and the Inmaculada Concepción Church in Guayanilla.

Also severely damaged by the January 7, 2020, quake was the La Guancha Recreational and Cultural Complex, which was made inoperable and where 24 establishments had to shut down their operations, and Auditorio Juan Pachín Vicen. The Moscoso Building of the Ponce City Hall was also damaged.

The January 11, 2020, aftershock inflicted further damage. Among the structures damaged by this aftershock were the Ponce Servicios municipal government building, Museo de la Masacre de Ponce, Residencia Armstrong-Poventud, and Casa Vives.

In Ponce both historic and modern buildings were damaged. Among these were Catedral de Nuestra Señora de Guadalupe, Museo de la Masacre, Iglesia Evangélica, northwest corner of Calle Unión and Calle Vives.

"La Gloria" store on Paseo Atocha, Hotel Ponce Plaza, Condominium Ponciana on C. Marina, Darlington Building, also on Calle Marina. The damages forced the closing of several downtown streets. There was also damage to Logia Aurora, also on Calle Marina.

Guanica and Yauco were particularly impacted. The Guanica lighthouse was among the buildings in that town with damage.

On January 11, 2020, Ponce alone had sustained an estimated $150 million in damages.

By 14 January 2020, the vice-mayor of Ponce estimated the cost of the damages so far in her town, one of the town's most severely hit at $1 billion. Financial losses were calculated at $3.1 billion US dollars.

The May 2, 2020, M 5.5 earthquake caused further damage to buildings in Ponce. Some power outages were also reported.

There was no electricity in Ponce and in most of Puerto Rico on Tuesday, January 7, 2020, the day of the 4:24AM earthquake. "More than 250,000" residents island-wide were left without water and another half a million had no power.

There were also rock and landslides. Among damage to infrastructure, the 5.9 aftershock quake the morning of January 11, 2020, created a crack in a bridge, and was expected to delay restoration of power.

The Costa Sur power plant, which provides a quarter of the island's power, had sustained "destruction on a grand scale" and estimates said it would take at least a year for repairs to be completed.

Consideration was being given the building a brand-new plant instead of repairing the damaged plant.

Road damages due to landslides included Puerto Rico highways PR-132, PR-139, and PR-218.

PR-2 had landslides in Peñón de Ponce; PR-9, a 4-lane highway under construction, had damages that set back the opening date several months; and PR-52 had damage to its Ponce toll booth plaza. Among bridges damaged were two on PR-127 in Guayanilla, at kilometer markers 9.1 and 10.3.

On January 17, 2020, Puerto Rico governor fired three members of her Cabinet after a group of Puerto Ricans broke into an enormous State warehouse in the La Guancha sector of Barrio Playa in Ponce and found it fully stocked with emergency items including cots, gas stoves, batteries, water, baby formula, diapers that had been stored there since after Hurricane Maria, and which the governor had not been made aware of.

The governor nominated the Adjutant General of the Puerto Rico National Guard to take over the post of fired Office of Emergency Management Secretary and ordered him to immediately move the items to the refugee centers of the municipalities affected by the earthquake and to distribute them to those people needing them.

The Puerto Rican Government contracted the services of nearly 50 structural engineers to evaluate each public school in the Island for structural stability post-earthquake and to certify them as safe enough to open. Classes were delayed more than 10 days Island-wide, longer in the two school regions most intensely hit by the earthquakes.

In the aftermath of the main quake and its major aftershocks, thousands of residents, including many whose homes had not been damaged, developed seismophobia and continued sleeping outdoors weeks after the earthquake of January 7, 2020.

On January 10, USGS and Puerto Rico Seismic Network, PRSN, scientists were working to install six sets of temporary seismometers near the southern coast to augment the existing PRSN instruments.

# CHAPTER 21

## Puerto Rico and the Virgin Islands

Puerto Rico and the Virgin Islands lie at the boundary between the Caribbean and North American plates, making these territories predisposed to earthquakes.

This is a highly active seismic region both surrounded and covered by numerous fault lines; to the north, the North American plate subducts into the Caribbean plate, while several transform fault lines cross the main island of Puerto Rico diagonally from southeast to northeast.

Puerto Rico and the Virgin Islands are also located on a microplate that is continuously being crushed by the subduction zone to the north. Puerto Rico is constantly prone to experiencing major earthquakes, superior to 7.0, at any moment.

The region has been seismically active since ancient times. The Great Northern and Great Southern fault zones that cross the main island of Puerto Rico laterally have been active since the Eocene epoch.

Earthquakes in the region have been recorded since the early 17th century and some of the first seismic activity in the Americas were recorded first in Puerto Rico and Hispaniola.

One of the first recorded earthquakes in the region was on September 8, 1615, which originated in the Dominican Republic region and caused damages throughout the island.

Earthquakes have been studied and recorded in Puerto Rico since the 20th century. The Puerto Rico Seismic Network, <u>Red Sísmica de Puerto Rico or RSPR</u>, which is contained within the department of

Geology of the University of Puerto Rico, Mayagüez, was established in 1974 by the United States Geological Survey, USGS, and the former Puerto Rico Electric Power Authority, PREPA.

It was established with the goal evaluating seismic features for the purpose of building nuclear power plants in the region. Its mission today is to detect, process and study seismic activity within the Puerto Rico region.

The RSPR operates 25 seismometers throughout Puerto Rico, the US Virgin Islands, and the British Virgin Islands. Two of these seismometers are owned by the United States Army Corps of Engineers.

On average, there are about 5 earthquakes recorded per day and about 3 earthquakes with magnitude 5.0 higher recorded per year in the region.

Given that most of the active faults are located at sea, most earthquakes in the region do not cause loss of life or significant damage, and significant destructive earthquakes that occur in Puerto Rico are rare. Most large earthquakes have historically occurred at sea which makes the area susceptible to destructive tsunamis.

The last tsunami to cause significant damages in Puerto Rico was on October 11, 1918. It generated by the 1918 Aguadilla earthquake. There have been more recent tsunami events, such as in 1946, which did not cause significant damage to the island.

The last earthquakes to cause loss of life were the 2020 southwestern Puerto Rico sequence of earthquakes which caused 4 deaths. The last earthquake to cause significant damage and loss of life in the Virgin Islands occurred in 1867; this earthquake generated a tsunami that affected the Virgin Islands and Puerto Rico.

# CHAPTER 22

# Earthquakes and Tsunamis in Barbados

Barbados is no stranger to earthquakes and tsunamis, and citizens are being urged to dispel the notion that they will not be impacted and become prepared.

Director of the University of the West Indies, Seismic Research Centre, Dr. Joan Latchman, is also warning that the region does have the capacity to generate big devastating events, as has happened in the past.

Speaking during a Tsunami Smart Teacher Training seminar at the Barbados Community College today, Dr. Latchman said over 500 earthquakes occurred within the Barbados seismic zone annually, with at least one occurring monthly in Barbados.

The perception that Barbados cannot be affected by earthquakes is wrong. Barbados is having earthquakes; there were earthquakes of a magnitude of five in 1981, 1984, and 1987 along Barbados.

The most recent one of a 6.4 magnitude near Martinique was felt.

Everyone was warned that earthquakes did not have to occur in Barbados to result in damage to the island. It just must be big enough.

In reference to an earthquake in 1953 off Barbados, caused significant damage in Bridgetown.

The 2007 earth tremor in Barbados saw reports of cracks in sidewalks and tiles falling from buildings. It showed that there can be infrastructural damage from the shaking.

Similarly, Barbadians the island was impacted by the 1755 Great Lisbon earthquake which resulted in a tsunami, and there was every possibility that the island could be impacted again in the future.

Everyone in Barbados needed to know and be aware and prepared for any eventuality earthquake.

Tsunamis were unpredictable hazards for which there is little or no warning.

Barbados is not a stranger to these kinds of impacts. If they happened in the past, know they can happen in the future. If they have a small earthquake, one day, there will be a big. if one sees small tsunamis, one day you will get a bigger one.

Dr. Latchman advised policy makers not to ignore the fact that earthquakes and tsunamis were a part of the Barbadian reality and should therefore be factored into the country's development plans.

The Director stressed that planners and stakeholders also needed to come together and decide on the appropriate response towards the hazards, as the measures to be taken depended heavily on what the priorities were for those involved.

# CHAPTER 23

# Jamaica 1692 earthquake

The 1692 Jamaica earthquake struck Port Royal, Jamaica, on 7 June. A stopped pocket watch found in the harbor during a 1959 excavation indicated that it occurred around 11:43 AM local time.

Known as the "storehouse and treasury of the West Indies" and as "one of the wickedest places on Earth", Port Royal was, at the time, the unofficial capital of Jamaica and one of the busiest and wealthiest ports in the Americas, as well as a common home port for many of the privateers and pirates operating on the Caribbean Sea.

The 1692 earthquake caused most of the city to sink below sea level. About 2,000 people died because of the earthquake.

The following tsunami, and another 3,000 people died in the following days due to injuries and disease.

The island of Jamaica lies on the boundary between the Caribbean Plate and the Gonâve Microplate. The Gonâve microplate is a 1,100 km, 680 mi, long strip of mainly oceanic crust formed by the Cayman spreading ridge within a strike-slip pull-apart basin on the northern transform margin of the Caribbean Plate with the North American Plate.

Jamaica was formed by uplift associated with a restraining bend along this strike-slip structure. The focal mechanisms of earthquakes around Jamaica are primarily sinistral strike-slip along WSW-ENE trending faults and minor reverse or thrust motion on NW-SE trending faults.

The 1692 event is thought to have occurred on one of these strike-slip faults.

Two-thirds of the town, about 13 ha, 33 acres, sank into the sea immediately after the main shock.

According to Robert Renny in his An History of Jamaica 1807. "All the docks sunk at once, and in the space of two minutes, nine-tenths of the city were covered with water, which was raised to such a height, that it entered the uppermost rooms of the few houses which were left standing. The tops of the highest houses were visible in the water and surrounded by the masts of vessels, which had been sunk along with them."

Before the earthquake the town consisted of 6,500 inhabitants living in about 2,000 buildings, many constructed of brick and with more than one level, and all built on loose sand.

During the shaking, the sand liquefied and the buildings, along with their occupants, appeared to flow into the sea. More than twenty ships anchored in the harbor were capsized.

One ship, the frigate Swann, was carried over the rooftops by the tsunami.

During the main shock, the sand was said to have formed waves. Fissures repeatedly opened and closed, crushing many people.

After the shaking stopped the sand again solidified, trapping many victims. Palisadoes cemetery, where the grave of the former pirate Sir Henry Morgan was located, was one of the parts of the city to fall into the sea; his body has never been found.

At Liguanea, present-day Kingston, all the houses were destroyed, and water was ejected from 12 m, 40-foot, deep wells. Almost all the houses at St. Jago, Spanish Town, were destroyed.

Many landslides occurred across the island. The largest, the Judgement Cliff landslide, displaced the land surface by up to 800 m and killed 19 people.

Several rivers were temporarily dammed and a few days after the earthquakes the harbor became flooded with large numbers of trees stripped of their bark brought down after one of these dams was breached.

A pocket watch, made in the Netherlands by the French maker Blondel in about 1686, was recovered during underwater archaeological investigations led by Edwin Link in 1959. The watch was stopped with its hands pointing to 11:43 AM; this matches well with contemporary accounts of the timing of the earthquake.

Even before the destruction was complete, some of the survivors began looting, breaking into homes and warehouses. The dead were also robbed and stripped, and, in some cases, had fingers cut off to remove the rings that they wore.

In the immediate aftermath of the earthquake, it was common to attribute the destruction to divine retribution on the people of Port Royal for their sinful ways.

Members of the Jamaica Council declared: "We are become by this an instance of God Almighty's severe judgement." This view of the disaster was not confined to Jamaica; in Boston, the Reverend Cotton Mather said in a letter to his uncle: "Behold, an accident speaking to all our English America".

After the earthquake, the town was partially rebuilt. But the colonial government was relocated to Spanish Town, which had been the capital under Spanish rule. Port Royal was devastated by a fire in 1703 and a hurricane in 1722.

Most of the sea trade moved to Kingston. By the late 18th century, Port Royal was largely abandoned.

There were three separate shocks, each with increasing intensity, culminating in the mainshock. The estimated size of the event was 7.5 on the moment magnitude scale.

Despite reports of the town flowing into the sea, the main result of the earthquake was subsidence caused by liquefaction. This would also explain an eyewitness account of houses being swallowed and people being buried up to their necks in the sand.

The probable triggering of the Judgement Cliff landslide during the earthquake occurred along the line of the Plantain Garden fault. Movement on this structure has been suggested as the cause of the earthquake.

The Judgement Cliff landslide is a complex rock-slide slump with a volume of about $131–181 \times 106$ m3. The slip surface is found within zones of clay and shale with gypsum at the base of a limestone unit.

This landslide occurred after the earthquake, but it remains possible that heavy rain over the few days after the event, or possibly during a hurricane in October later that year was the final trigger for the slip.

The sea was observed to retreat by about 300 yd, 270 m, at Liguanea. This was probably near Kingston. While at Yallahs, it withdrew 1 mi, 1.6 km. It returned as a 6 ft, 1.8 m, high wave that swept over the land.

One possible cause of the tsunami is thought to be the slump and grain flow into the harbor from beneath the town itself, although the waves in the harbor may be better described as seiches and larger waves reported elsewhere, such as at Saint Ann's Bay, are explained as the result of an entirely separate submarine landslide, also triggered by the earthquake.

Estimates of current deformation of Jamaica suggest that sufficient strain has accumulated to generate a M=7.0–7.3 earthquake, similar in size to the 1692 event.

This may mean that a repeat of this event is pending, although this estimate relies on many assumptions, such as that none of the motion on the Plantain Garden fault is accommodated by aseismic creep.

# CHAPTER 24

# Cuba

Cuba is in an area with several active fault systems which produce on average about 2000 seismic events each year.

Cuba earthquake hazard is classified as medium according to the information that is currently available. This means that there is a 10% chance of potentially damaging earthquake shaking in your project area in the next 50 years.

Based on this information, the impact of earthquake should be considered in all phases of the project, during design and construction. Project planning decisions, project design, and construction methods should consider the level of earthquake hazard.

While most registered seismic events pass unnoticed, the island has been struck by several destructive earthquakes over the past four centuries, including several major quakes with a magnitude of 7.0 or above.

Approximately 70% of seismic activity in Cuba emanates from the Oriente fault zone, located in the Bartlett-Cayman fault system which runs along the south-eastern coast of Cuba and marks the tectonic boundary between the North American Plate and the Caribbean Plate.

The 12 currently active faults in Cuba also include the Cauto-Nipe, Cochinos and Mortician faults.

Destructive earthquakes originating from the Oriente fault occurred in 1766, MI= 7.6, 1852 MI = 7.2 and 1932Ms = 6.75.

Some studies suggested there is a high probability the Oriente fault would produce a magnitude 7 earthquake, this happening in January 2020, with a magnitude of 7.7, the highest registered in this country's history.

# CHAPTER 25

## Dominican Republic

### The Septentrional-Oriente fault zone in the Caribbean and across Hispaniola

The 1946 Dominican Republic earthquake occurred on August 4 at 17:51 UTC near Samaná, Dominican Republic. The mainshock measured 7.8 on the moment magnitude scale and 8.1 on the surface wave magnitude scale.

An aftershock occurred four days later August 8 at 13:28 UTC with a moment magnitude of 7.0.

A tsunami was generated by the initial earthquake and caused widespread devastation across Hispaniola. The tsunami was observed in much of the Caribbean and the northwestern Atlantic Ocean.

A small tsunami was also recorded by tide gauges at San Juan in Puerto Rico, Bermuda and in the United States at Daytona Beach, Florida, and Atlantic City.

### Natural disasters Hurricanes

The Atlantic hurricane season runs from June to November. In the Caribbean this frequently coincides with heavy rains, which may cause flash floods and landslides. You should monitor local and international weather updates from the US National Hurricane Centre and follow the advice of local authorities and your tour operator.

Hurricanes Irma and Maria caused some local flooding and minor damage to buildings in the north and east of the country in September 2017.

There are occasional earthquakes in the Dominican Republic. To protect yourself during an earthquake, you should drop to the ground, take cover, and hold on until the shaking stops. If you're inside a building don't exist until it's safe to do so. If you're outside, move away from buildings, streetlights, and electricity wires.

After the earthquake don't run as there may be aftershocks or debris in your path. If you become trapped, tap on a pipe or wall so rescuers can find you. Only shout as a last resort as this may cause you to inhale dust. In the event of an earthquake, the Dominican Government authorities, fire-fighters, and police will provide help to foreigners.

If a major earthquake occurs close to shore, you should follow the instructions of the local authorities, bearing in mind that a tsunami could arrive within minutes.

The US Federal Emergency Management Agency has advice about what to do before during and after an earthquake and tsunami

# CHAPTER 26

## 2010 Haiti earthquake

A catastrophic magnitude 7.0 Mw earthquake struck Haiti at 16:53 local time, 21:53 UTC, on Tuesday, 12 January 2010. The epicenter was near the town of Léogâne, Ouest department, approximately twenty-five kilometers,16 mi, west of Port-au-Prince, Haiti's capital.

By 24 January, at least 52 aftershocks measuring 4.5 or greater had been recorded. An estimated three million people were affected by the quake.

Death toll estimates range from 100,000 to about 160,000 to Haitian government figures from 220,000 to 316,000, although these latter figures are a matter of some dispute.

The government of Haiti estimated that 250,000 residences and 30,000 commercial buildings had collapsed or were severely damaged.

The nation's history of national debt, prejudicial trade policies by other countries, and foreign intervention into national affairs contributed to the existing poverty and poor housing conditions that increased the death toll from the disaster.

The earthquake caused major damage in Port-au-Prince, Jacmel and other cities in the region. Notable landmark buildings were significantly damaged or destroyed, including the Presidential Palace, the National Assembly building, the Port-au-Prince Cathedral, and the main jail. Among those killed were Archbishop of Port-au-Prince Joseph Serge Miot, and opposition leader Micha Gaillard.

The headquarters of the United Nations Stabilization Mission in Haiti, MINUSTAH, located in the capital, collapsed, killing many, including the Mission's Chief, Hédi Annabi.

Many countries responded to appeals for humanitarian aid, pledging funds and dispatching rescue and medical teams, engineers, and support personnel. The most-watched telethon in history aired on 22 January, called "Hope for Haiti Now," raising U.S. $58 million by the next day.

Communication systems, air, land, and sea transport facilities, hospitals, and electrical networks had been damaged by the earthquake, which hampered rescue and aid efforts; confusion over who was in charge, air traffic congestion, and problems with ordering flights further complicated early relief work.

Port-au-Prince's morgues were overwhelmed with tens of thousands of bodies. These had to be buried in mass graves.

As rescues tailed off, supplies, medical care and sanitation became priorities. Delays in aid distribution led to angry appeals from aid workers and survivors and looting and sporadic violence were observed.

On 22 January, the United Nations noted that the emergency phase of the relief operation was ending, and on the following day, the Haitian government officially called off the search for survivors.

The island of Hispaniola, shared by Haiti and the Dominican Republic, is seismically active and has a history of destructive earthquakes. During Haiti's time as a French colony, earthquakes were recorded by French historian Moreau de Saint-Mary, 1750–1819.

He described damage done by an earthquake in 1751, writing that "only one masonry building had not collapsed" in Port-au-Prince; he also wrote that the "whole city collapsed" in the 1770 Port-au-Prince earthquake.

Cap-Haïtien, other towns in the north of Haiti and the Dominican Republic, and the Sans-Souci Palace were destroyed during an earthquake on 7 May 1842.

A magnitude 8.0 earthquake struck the Dominican Republic and shook Haiti on 4 August 1946, producing a tsunami that killed 1,790 people and injured many others.

Haiti is the poorest country in the Western Hemisphere and is ranked 149th of 182 countries on the Human Development Index.

The Australian government's travel advisory site had previously expressed concerns that Haitian emergency services would be unable to cope in the event of a major disaster, and the country is considered "economically vulnerable" by the Food and Agriculture Organization.

Haiti is no stranger to natural disasters. In addition to earthquakes, it has been struck frequently by tropical cyclones, which have caused flooding and widespread damage. The most recent cyclones to hit the island before the earthquake were Tropical Storm Fay and Hurricanes Gustav, Hanna, and Ike, all in the summer of 2008, causing nearly 800 deaths.

he magnitude 7.0 Mw earthquake occurred inland, on 12 January 2010 at 16:53, UTC–05:00, approximately 25 km, 16 mi, WSW from Port-au-Prince at a depth of 13 km, 8.1 mi, on blind thrust faults associated with the Enriquillo-Plantain Garden fault system and lasted less than 30 seconds.

There is no evidence of surface rupture; based on seismological, geological, and ground deformation data, it is also thought that the earthquake did not involve significant lateral slip on the main Enriquillo fault.

Strong shaking associated with intensity IX on the Modified Mercalli scale (MM) was recorded in Port-au-Prince and its suburbs. It was also felt in several surrounding countries and regions, including Cuba MM III in Guantánamo, Jamaica MM II in Kingston, Venezuela MM II in Caracas, Puerto Rico MM II–III in San Juan), and the bordering Dominican Republic, MM III in Santo Domingo.

According to estimates from the U.S. Geological Survey, approximately 3.5 million people lived in the area that experienced shaking intensity of MM VII to X, a range that can cause moderate to very heavy damage even to earthquake-resistant structures. Shaking damage was more severe than for other quakes of similar magnitude due to the quake's shallow depth.

The quake occurred in the vicinity of the northern boundary where the Caribbean tectonic plate shifts eastwards by about 20 mm, 0.79 in, per year in relation to the North American plate.

The strike-slip fault system in the region has two branches in Haiti, the Septentrional-Oriente fault in the north and the Enriquillo-Plantain

Garden fault in the south; both its location and focal mechanism suggested that the January 2010 quake was caused by a rupture of the Enriquillo-Plantain Garden fault, which had been locked for 250 years, gathering stress.

However, a study published in May 2010 suggested that the rupture process may have involved slip on multiple blind thrust faults with only minor, deep, lateral slip along or near the main Enriquillo–Plantain Garden fault zone, suggesting that the event only partially relieved centuries of accumulated left-lateral strain on a small part of the plate-boundary system.

The rupture was roughly 65 km (40 mi) long with mean slip of 1.8 meters, 5 ft 11 in.

Preliminary analysis of the slip distribution found amplitudes of up to about 4 m, 13 ft, using ground motion records from all over the world.

A 2007 earthquake hazard study by C. Dements and M. Wiggins-Grandison noted that the Enriquillo-Plantain Garden fault zone could be at the end of its seismic cycle and concluded that a worst-case forecast would involve a 7.2 Mw earthquake, similar in size to the 1692 Jamaica earthquake.

Paul Mann and a group including the 2006 study team presented a hazard assessment of the Enriquillo-Plantain Garden fault system to the 18th Caribbean Geologic Conference in March 2008, noting the large strain; the team recommended "high priority" historical geologic rupture studies, as the fault was fully locked and had recorded few earthquakes in the preceding 40 years.

An article published in Haiti's Le Matin newspaper in September 2008 cited comments by geologist Patrick Charles to the effect that there was a high risk of major seismic activity in Port-au-Prince.

The U.S. Geological Survey recorded eight aftershocks in the two hours after the main earthquake, with magnitudes between 4.3 and 5.9.

Within the first nine hours, 32 aftershocks of magnitude 4.2 or greater were recorded, 12 of which measured magnitude 5.0 or greater; in addition, on 24 January, the US Geological Survey reported that there had been 52 aftershocks measuring 4.5 or greater since the main quake.

On 20 January, at 06:03 local time 11:03 UTC, the strongest aftershock since the earthquake, measuring magnitude 5.9 Mw, struck Haiti.

USGS reported its epicenter was about 56 km, 35 mi, WSW of Port-au-Prince, which would place it almost exactly under the coastal town of Petit-Goave. A UN representative reported that the aftershock collapsed seven buildings in the town.

According to staff of the International Committee of the Red Cross, which had reached Petit-Goâve for the first time the day before the aftershock, the town was estimated to have lost 15% of its buildings and was suffering the same shortages of supplies and medical care as the capital.

Workers from the charity Save the Children reported hearing "already weakened structures collapsing" in Port-au-Prince, but most sources reported no further significant damage to infrastructure in the city. Further casualties are thought to have been minimal since people had been sleeping in the open.

There are concerns that the main earthquake could be the beginning of a new long-term sequence: "the whole region is fearful"; historical accounts, although not precise, suggest that there has been a sequence of quakes progressing westwards along the fault, starting with an earthquake in the Dominican Republic in 1751.

The Pacific Tsunami Warning Center issued a tsunami warning immediately after the initial quake, but quickly cancelled it.

Nearly two weeks later it was reported that the beach of the small fishing town of Petit Paradis was hit by a localized tsunami shortly after the earthquake, probably because of an underwater landslide, and this was later confirmed by researchers.

At least three people were swept out to sea by the wave and were reported dead. Witnesses told reporters that the sea first retreated, and a "very big wave" followed rapidly, crashing ashore and sweeping boats and debris into the ocean. The tsunami reached heights up to 3 m. 9.8 ft.

Amongst the widespread devastation and damage throughout Port-au-Prince and elsewhere, vital infrastructure necessary to respond to the disaster was severely damaged or destroyed. This included all hospitals in the capital; air, sea, and land transport facilities; and communication systems.

The quake affected the three Médecins Sans Frontières, Doctors Without Borders, medical facilities around Port-au-Prince, causing one to collapse completely.

A hospital in Pétion-Ville, a wealthy suburb of Port-au-Prince, also collapsed, as did the St. Michel District Hospital in the southern town of Jacmel, which was the largest referral hospital in south-east Haiti.

he quakes seriously damaged the control tower at Toussaint L'Ouverture International Airport.

Damage to the Port-au-Prince seaport rendered the harbor unusable for immediate rescue operations; its container crane subsided severely at an angle because of weak foundations. Gonaïves seaport in northern Haiti remained operational.

Roads were blocked with road rubble, or the surfaces broken. The main road linking Port-au-Prince with Jacmel remained blocked ten days after the earthquake, hampering delivery of aid to Jacmel. When asked why the road had not been opened, Hazem el-Zein, head of the south-east division of the UN World Food Programme said that "We ask the same questions to the people in charge...

They promise rapid response. To be honest, I don't know why it hasn't been done. I can only think that their priority must be somewhere else."

There was considerable damage to communications infrastructure.

The public telephone system was not available, and two of Haiti's largest cellular telephone providers, Digicel and Comcel Haiti, both reported that their services had been affected by the earthquake. Fibre-optic connectivity was also disrupted.

According to Reporters Sans Frontières, RSF, Radio Lumière, which broadcasts out of Port-au-Prince and reaches 90% of Haiti, was initially knocked off the air, but it was able to resume broadcasting across most of its network within a week.

According to RSF, some 20 of about 50 stations that were active in the capital region before the earthquake were back on air a week after the quake.

In February 2010 Prime Minister Jean-Max Bellerive estimated that 250,000 residences and 30,000 commercial buildings were severely damaged and needed to be demolished.

The deputy mayor of Léogâne reported that 90% of the town's buildings had been destroyed. Many government and public buildings were damaged or destroyed including the Palace of Justice, the National Assembly, the Supreme Court, and Port-au-Prince Cathedral.

The National Palace was severely damaged, though President René Préval and his wife Elisabeth Delatour Préval escaped without injury.

The Prison Civile de Port-au-Prince was also destroyed, allowing around 4,000 inmates to escape.

Most of Port-au-Prince's municipal buildings were destroyed or heavily damaged, including the City Hall, which was described by The Washington Post as, "a skeletal hulk of concrete and stucco, sagging grotesquely to the left."

Port-au-Prince had no municipal petrol reserves and few city officials had working mobile phones before the earthquake, making communications and transportation very difficult.

Minister of Education Joel Jean-Pierre stated that the education system had "totally collapsed". About half the nation's schools and the three main universities in Port-au-Prince were affected. More than 1,300 schools and 50 health care facilities were destroyed.

The earthquake also destroyed a nursing school in the capital and severely damaged the country's primary midwifery school.

The Haitian art world suffered great losses; artworks were destroyed, and museums and art galleries were extensively damaged, among them Port-au-Prince's main art museum, Centre d'Art school, College Saint Pierre, and Holy Trinity Cathedral.

The headquarters of the United Nations Stabilization Mission in Haiti (MINUSTAH) at Christopher Hotel and offices of the World Bank were destroyed.

The building housing the offices of Citibank in Port-au-Prince collapsed, killing five employees. The clothing industry, which accounts for two-thirds of Haiti's exports, reported structural damage at manufacturing facilities.

The quake created a landslide dam on the Rivière de Grand Goâve. As of February 2010, the water level was low, but engineer Yves Gattereau believed the dam could collapse during the rainy season, which would flood Grand-Goâve 12 km (7.5 mi) downstream.

In the nights following the earthquake, many people in Haiti slept in the streets, on pavements, in their cars, or in makeshift shanty towns either because their houses had been destroyed, or they feared standing structures would not withstand aftershocks.

Construction standards are low in Haiti; the country has no building codes. Engineers have stated that it is unlikely many buildings would have stood through any kind of disaster. Structures are often raised wherever they can fit; some buildings were built on slopes with insufficient foundations or steel supports.

A representative of Catholic Relief Services has estimated that about two million Haitians lived as squatters on land they did not own. The country also suffered from shortages of fuel and potable water even before the disaster.

President Préval and government ministers used police headquarters near the Toussaint L'Ouverture International Airport as their new base of operations, although their effectiveness was extremely limited; several parliamentarians were still trapped in the Presidential Palace, and offices and records had been destroyed.

Some high-ranking government workers lost family members or had to tend to wound relatives. Although the president and his remaining cabinet met with UN planners each day, there remained confusion as to who was in charge and no single group had organized relief efforts as of 16 January.

The government handed over control of the airport to the United States to hasten and ease flight operations, which had been hampered by the damage to the air traffic control tower.

Almost immediately Port-au-Prince's morgue facilities were overwhelmed. By 14 January, a thousand bodies had been placed on the streets and pavements. Government crews manned trucks to collect thousands more, burying them in mass graves.

In the heat and humidity, corpses buried in rubble began to decompose and smell. Mati Goldstein, head of the Israeli ZAKA

International Rescue Unit delegation to Haiti, described the situation as "Shabbat from hell. Everywhere, the acrid smell of bodies hangs in the air.

It's just like the stories we are told of the Holocaust—thousands of bodies everywhere. You must understand that the situation is true madness, and the more time passes, there are more and more bodies, in numbers that cannot be grasped. It is beyond comprehension."

Mayor Jean-Yves Jason said that officials argued for hours about what to do with the volume of corpses. The government buried many in mass graves, some above-ground tombs were forced open so bodies could be stacked inside, and others were burned.

Mass graves were dug in a large field outside the settlement of Titanyen, north of the capital; tens of thousands of bodies were reported as having been brought to the site by dump truck and buried in trenches dug by earth movers.

Max Beauvoir, a Vodou priest, protested the lack of dignity in mass burials, stating, "… it is not in our culture to bury people in such a fashion, it is desecration".

Towns in the eastern Dominican Republic began preparing for tens of thousands of refugees, and by 16 January hospitals close to the border had been filled with Haitians.

Some began reporting having expended stocks of critical medical supplies such as antibiotics by 17 January.

The border was reinforced by Dominican soldiers, and the government of the Dominican Republic asserted that all Haitians who crossed the border for medical assistance would be allowed to stay only temporarily. A local governor stated, "We have a great desire, and we will do everything humanly possible to help Haitian families. But we have our limitations with respect to food and medicine. We need the helping hand of other countries in the area."

Slow distribution of resources in the days after the earthquake resulted in sporadic violence, with looting reported.

There were also accounts of looters wounded or killed by vigilantes and neighborhoods that had constructed their own roadblock barricades.

Dr Evan Lyon of Partners in Health, working at the General Hospital in Port-au-Prince, claimed that misinformation and overblown reports of violence had hampered the delivery of aid and medical services.

Former US president Bill Clinton acknowledged the problems and said Americans should "not be deterred from supporting the relief effort" by upsetting scenes such as those of looting.

Lt. Gen. P.K. Keen, deputy commander of US Southern Command, however, announced that despite the stories of looting and violence, there was less violent crime in Port-au-Prince after the earthquake than before.

In many neighborhoods, singing could be heard through the night and groups of men coordinated to act as security as groups of women attempted to take care of food and hygiene necessities.

During the days following the earthquake, hundreds were seen marching through the streets in peaceful processions, singing and clapping.

The earthquake caused an urgent need for outside rescuers to communicate with Haitians whose main or only language is Haitian Creole. As a result, a mobile translation program to translate between English and Haitian Creole had to be written quickly.

The generation of waste from relief operations was referred to as a "second disaster". The United States military reported that millions of water bottles and Styrofoam food packages were distributed although there was no operational waste management system.

Over 700,000 plastic tarpaulins and 100,000 tents were required for emergency shelters. The increase in plastic waste, combined with poor disposal practices, resulted in open drainage channels being blocked, increasing the risk of disease.

The earthquake struck in the most populated area of the country. The International Federation of Red Cross and Red Crescent Societies estimated that as many as 3 million people had been affected by the quake.[11] In mid-February 2010, the Haitian government reported the death toll to have reached 230,000.

However, an investigation by Radio Netherlands has questioned the official death toll, reporting an estimate of 92,000 deaths as being a more realistic figure.

On the first anniversary of the earthquake, 12 January 2011, Haitian Prime Minister Jean-Max Bellerive said the death toll from the quake was more than 316,000, raising the figures from previous estimates.

Several experts have questioned the validity of the death toll numbers; Anthony Penna, professor emeritus in environmental history at Northeastern University, warned that casualty estimates could only be a "guesstimate", and Belgian disaster response expert Claude de Ville de Goyet noted that "round numbers are a sure sign that nobody knows."

Edmond Mulet, UN Assistant Secretary-General for Peacekeeping Operations, said, "I do not think we will ever know what the death toll is from this earthquake", while the director of the Haitian Red Cross, Jean-Pierre Guiteau, noted that his organization had not had the time to count bodies, as their focus had been on the treatment of survivors.

While most casualties were Haitian civilians, the dead included aid workers, embassy staff, foreign tourists—and several public figures, including Archbishop of Port-au-Prince Monsignor Joseph Serge Miot, aid worker Zilda Arns and officials in the Haitian government, including opposition leader Michel "Micha" Gaillard.

Also killed were several well-known Haitian musicians and sports figures, including thirty members of the Fédération Haïtienne de Football.

At least 85 United Nations personnel working with MINUSTAH were killed, among them the Mission Chief, Hédi Annabi, his deputy, Luiz Carlos da Costa, and police commissioner Douglas Coates.

About 200 guests were killed in the collapse of the Hôtel Montana in Port-au-Prince.

On 31 May 2011, an unreleased draft report based on a survey commissioned by the US Agency for International Development (USAID) challenged the Haiti earthquake death toll and several damage estimates.

The unpublished report put the death toll between 46,000 and 85,000 and put the number of displaced persons at 895,000, of which only 375,000 remained in temporary shelters. The unreleased report, which compiled its figures from a door-to-door survey, was done by a Washington consulting firm, LTL Strategies.

A US State Department spokesperson said the report had inconsistencies and would not be released until they were resolved. As of January 2012, USAID has not released the report and states on its website that 1.5 million people were displaced, of which 550,000 remain without permanent shelter.

The most reliable academic estimate of the number of earthquake casualties in Haiti (over 95% were in the immediate Port-au-Prince area) "within six weeks of the earthquake" appears to be the 160,000 estimate in a 2010 University of Michigan study.

Appeals for humanitarian aid were issued by many aid organizations, the United Nation and President René Préval. Raymond Joseph, Haiti's ambassador to the United States, and his nephew, singer Wyclef Jean, [who was called upon by Préval to become a "roving ambassador" for Haiti, also pleaded for aid and donations. Images and testimonials circulating after the earthquake across the internet and through social media helped to intensify the reaction of global engagement.

Many countries responded to the appeals and launched fund-raising efforts, as well as sending search and rescue teams. The neighboring Dominican Republic was the first country to give aid to Haiti, sending water, food, and heavy-lifting machinery.

The hospitals in the Dominican Republic were made available; a combined effort of the Airports Department (DA), together with the Dominican Naval Auxiliaries, the UN and other parties formed the Dominican-Haitian Aerial Support Bridge, making the main Dominican airports available for support operations to Haiti.

The Dominican website FlyDominicanRepublic.com made available to the internet, daily updates on airport information and news from the operations center on the Dominican side.

The Dominican emergency team assisted more than 2,000 injured people, while the Dominican Institute of Telecommunications helped with the restoration of some telephone services.

The Dominican Red Cross coordinated early medical relief in conjunction with the International Red Cross. The government sent eight mobile medical units along with 36 doctors including orthopedic specialists, traumatologists, anesthetists, and surgeons.

In addition, 39 trucks carrying canned food were dispatched, along with 10 mobile kitchens and 110 cooks capable of producing 100,000 meals per day.

Other nations from farther afield also sent personnel, medicines, materiel, and other aid to Haiti. The first team to arrive in Port-au-Prince was ICE-SAR from Iceland, landing within 24 hours of the earthquake A 50-member Chinese team arrived early Thursday morning From the Middle East, the government of Qatar sent a strategic transport aircraft (C-17), loaded with 50 tons of urgent relief materials and 26 members from the Qatari armed forces, the internal security force (Lukwiya), police force and the Hamad Medical Corporation, to set up a field hospital and provide assistance in Port-au-Prince and other affected areas in Haiti.

A rescue team sent by the Israel Defense Forces' Home Front Command established a field hospital near the United Nations building in Port-au-Prince with specialized facilities to treat children, the elderly, and women in labor. It was set up in eight hours and began operations on the evening of 16 January.

A Korean International Disaster Relief Team with 40 rescuers, medical doctors, nurses and 2 k-9s was deployed to epicenters to assist mitigation efforts of Haitian Government.

The American Red Cross announced on 13 January that it had run out of supplies in Haiti and appealed for public donations. Giving Children Hope worked to get much-needed medicines and supplies on the ground.

Partners in Health (PIH), the largest health care provider in rural Haiti, was able to provide some emergency care from its ten hospitals and clinics, all of which were outside the capital and undamaged.

MINUSTAH had over 9,000 uniformed peacekeepers deployed to the area.[135] Most of these workers were initially involved in the search for survivors at the organization's collapsed headquarters.

The International Charter on Space and Major Disasters was activated, allowing satellite imagery of affected regions to be shared with rescue and aid organizations.

Members of social networking sites such as Twitter and Facebook spread messages and pleas to send help. Facebook was overwhelmed by and blocked some users who were sending messages about updates.

The American Red Cross set a record for mobile donations, raising US$7 million in 24 hours when they allowed people to send US$10 donations by text messages.

The OpenStreetMap community responded to the disaster by greatly improving the level of mapping available for the area using post-earthquake satellite photography provided by GeoEye, and crowdmapping website Ushahidi coordinated messages from multiple sites to assist Haitians still trapped and to keep families of survivors informed.

Some online poker sites hosted poker tournaments with tournament fees, prizes or both going to disaster relief charities.

Google Earth updated its coverage of Port-au-Prince on 17 January, showing the earthquake-ravaged city.

Easing refugee immigration into Canada was discussed by Canadian Prime Minister Stephen Harper, and in the US Haitians were granted Temporary protected status, a measure that permits about 100,000 illegal alien Haitians in the United States to stay legally for 18 months, and halts the deportations of 30,000 more, though it does not apply to Haitians outside the US.

Local and state agencies in South Florida, together with the US government, began implementing a plan, "Operation Vigilant Sentry", for a mass migration from the Caribbean that had been laid out in 2003.

Several orphanages were destroyed in the earthquake. After the process for the adoption of 400 children by families in the US and the Netherlands was expedited, UNICEF and SOS Children urged an immediate halt to adoptions from Haiti Jasmine Whitbread, chief executive of Save the Children said: "The vast majority of the children currently on their own still have family members alive who will be desperate to be reunited with them and will be able to care for them with the right support.

Taking children out of the country would permanently separate thousands of children from their families, a separation that would compound the acute trauma they are already suffering and inflict long-term damage on their chances of recovery.

However, several organizations were planning an airlift of thousands of orphaned children to South Florida on humanitarian visas, modelled on a similar effort with Cuban refugees in the 1960s named "Pedro Pan".

On 29 January 2010, a group of ten American Baptist missionaries from Idaho attempted to cross the Haiti-Dominican Republic border with 33 Haitian children. The group, known as the New Life Children's Refuge, did not have proper authorization for transporting the children and were arrested on kidnapping charges.

The Canadian government worked to expedite around 100 adoption cases that were already underway when the earthquake struck, issuing temporary permits, and waiving regular processing fees; the federal government also announced that it would cover adopted children's healthcare costs upon their arrival in Canada until they could be covered under provincially administered public healthcare plans.

Rescue efforts began in the immediate aftermath of the earthquake, with able-bodied survivors extricating the living and the dead from the rubble of the many buildings that had collapsed.

Treatment of the injured was hampered by the lack of hospital and morgue facilities: the Argentine military field hospital, which had been serving MINUSTAH, was the only one available until 13 January.

Rescue work intensified only slightly with the arrival of doctors, police officers, military personnel, and firefighters from various countries two days after the earthquake.

The International Charter on Space and Major Disasters was activated, allowing satellite imagery of affected regions to be shared with rescue and aid organizations.

Members of social networking sites such as Twitter and Facebook spread messages and pleas to send help. Facebook was overwhelmed by— and blocked—some users who were sending messages about updates.

The American Red Cross set a record for mobile donations, raising U.S. $7 million in 24 hours when they allowed people to send US$10 donations by text messages.

The OpenStreetMap community responded to the disaster by greatly improving the level of mapping available for the area using post-earthquake satellite photography provided by GeoEye, and crowd mapping website Ushahidi coordinated messages from multiple sites to assist Haitians still trapped and to keep families of survivors informed.

Some online poker sites hosted poker tournaments with tournament fees, prizes or both going to disaster relief charities.

U.S. President Barack Obama announced that former presidents Bill Clinton, who also acts as the UN special envoy to Haiti, and George W. Bush would coordinate efforts to raise funds for Haiti's recovery.

Secretary of State Hillary Clinton visited Haiti on 16 January to survey the damage and stated that U.S. $48 million had been raised already in the US to help Haiti recover.

Following the meeting with Secretary Clinton, President Préval stated that the highest priorities in Haiti's recovery were establishing a working government, clearing roads, and ensuring the streets were cleared of bodies to improve sanitary conditions.

U.S. Vice President Joe Biden stated on 16 January that President Obama "does not view this as a humanitarian mission with a life cycle of a month. This will still be on our radar screen long after it's off the crawler at CNN. This is going to be a long slog."

A remake of the song "Wavin' Flag" by Somalian-Canadian singer K'naan became a charity single in Canada, reaching number 1 on the "Canadian Hot 100" chart. The song was later chosen as Coca-Cola's promotional anthem for the 2010 FIFA World Cup hosted by South Africa.

Trade and Industry Minister Joseline Colimon Fethiere estimated that the earthquake's toll on the Haitian economy would be massive, with one in five jobs lost.

In response to the earthquake, foreign governments offered badly needed financial aid. The European Union promised €330 million for emergency and long-term aid. Brazil announced R$375 million for long-term recovery aid, R$25 million of which in immediate funds.

The United Kingdom's Secretary of State for International Development Douglas Alexander called the result of the earthquake an "almost unprecedented level of devastation", and committed the UK to £20 million in aid, while France promised €10 million.

Italy announced it would waive repayment of the €40 million it had loaned to Haiti, and the World Bank waived the country's debt repayments for five years.

On 14 January, the US government announced it would give US$100 million to the aid effort and pledged that the people of Haiti "will not be forgotten".

Six months after the quake as much as 98% of the rubble remained uncleared. An estimated 26 million cubic yards, 20 million cubic meters remained, making most of the capital impassable, and thousands of bodies remained in the rubble.

The number of people in relief camps of tents and tarps since the quake was 1.6 million, and almost no transitional housing had been built. Most of the camps had no electricity, running water, or sewage disposal, and the tents were beginning to fall apart. Crime in the camps was widespread, especially against women and girls. Between 23 major charities, US$1.1 billion had been collected for Haiti for relief efforts, but only two percent of the money had been released.

According to a CBS report, US$3.1 billion had been pledged for humanitarian aid and was used to pay for field hospitals, plastic tarps, bandages, and food, plus salaries, transportation, and upkeep of relief workers.

By May 2010, enough aid had been raised internationally to give each displaced family a cheque for US$37,000.

In July 2010, CNN returned to Port-au-Prince and reported, "It looks like the quake just happened yesterday", and Imogen Wall, spokeswoman for the United Nations office of humanitarian affairs in Haiti, said that "six months from that time it may still look the same."

Land ownership posed a particular problem for rebuilding because so many pre-quake homes were not officially registered.

Haitian grassroots groups advocated for the government to fulfill the right to housing as designated in the Haitian constitution, and for donor governments to support this as well.

They also worked to push the international community to recognize the wave of evictions from camps that started as early as three months after the earthquake and to put protections in place, but little was done in response.

In September 2010, there were over one million refugees still living in tents, and the humanitarian situation was characterized as still being in the emergency phase, according to the Apostolic Nuncio to Haiti, Archbishop Bernard Auza.

He went on to say that the number was rising instead of diminishing and reported that the state had decided to first rebuild downtown Port-au-Prince and a new government center, but reconstruction had not yet begun.

In October 2010, Refugees International characterized the aid agencies as dysfunctional and inexperienced saying, "The people of Haiti are still living in a state of emergency, with a humanitarian response that appears paralyzed". It was reported that gang leaders and landowners were intimidating the displaced and that sexual, domestic, and gang violence in and around the camps was rising.

They claimed that rape of Haitian women and girls who had been living in camps since the January earthquake were increasing, in part, because the United Nations wasn't doing enough to protect them.

In October, a cholera epidemic broke out, probably introduced by United Nations peacekeepers. Cholera most often affects poor countries with limited access to clean water and proper sanitation.

By the end of 2010, more than 3,333 had died at a rate of about 50 deaths a day.

In January 2011, one year after the quake, Oxfam published a report on the status of the recovery. According to the report, relief and recovery were at a standstill due to government inaction and indecision on the part of the donor countries.

The report stated:

"One year on, only five percent of the rubble has been cleared and only 15 percent of the required basic and temporary houses have been built. House building on a large scale cannot be started before the enormous amount of rubble is cleared. The government and donors must prioritize this most basic step toward helping people return home".

# CHAPTER 27

## Puerto Rico's Nature Rage

When hurricanes Irma and Maria barreled across Puerto Rico during the 2017 hurricane season, the storms left homes damaged in their wake and exacerbated longstanding.

The persistent housing issues and challenges can be seen all over the island. Habitat for Humanity responded in the immediate aftermath by assessing the damage and providing shelter kits and solar kits to affected families.

Hurricane María left a path of destruction as it passed over Puerto Rico the night of September 20th, 2017. The island lost most of its essential services' infrastructure, entire communities were leveled, thousands died and there were many more refugees.

Four years after the biggest disaster in Puerto Rico's modern history, the reconstruction of the island's infrastructure has still to get underway."

"After four years, every piece of the puzzle has fall into place," said Manuel Laboy. Executive director of the Central Office for Recovery, Reconstruction and Resilience.

"Much has been done so far, and I understand there is much still to be done, but emergency projects needed to be done before the reconstruction could begin," added Laboy, who admitted there are still more than 2,800 infrastructure projects without any obligated budget from the Federal Emergency Management Administration, FEMA.

Laboy explained that during these last four years the different government agencies involved in Puerto Rico's recovery process have

"established the conditions for the execution" for the recovery and reconstruction of the island.

During this time, according to Laboy, FEMA, the COR3, Commonwealth and municipal entities have engaged in "the stabilization, recovery planning, emergency and small project development," to create the conditions to start executing the permanent projects for Puerto Rico's definitive recovery.

Laboy also highlighted the fact that the whole process was further compounded by the 2020 earthquakes on the southwestern part of the island and the Covid-19 pandemic.

After the change in administration, Laboy said COR3's priorities and strategic goals were "revisited and updated to align them with then recently sworn Governor Pedro Pierluisi's public policies, and FEMA's execution, efficiency, compliance, and transparency directives.

While he admitted that FEMA and COR3 processes could be characterized as "lengthy and bureaucratic," Laboy insisted on their need and assured significant progress has been made.

"You have to realize that, of the $32.1 billion requested for the reconstruction, $27.9 billion have already been obligated", he pointed out. Laboy specified that $19.3 billion of the obligated funds have been allocated for permanent works.

Those projects are mainly for the Electric Power and Aqueduct and Sewer authorities, municipal governments, and the Department of Education., with the two public corporations taking the biggest share, $13.2 billion, PREPA $9.5 billion and PRASA $3.7 billion, or 68% of the obligated funds. Municipal governments and the Department of Education were allotted $2.1 billion and $2 billion respectively.

The rest of the $19.3 billion were distributed among the University of Puerto Rico, The Department of Transportation and Public Works, the Puerto Rico Industrial Development Corporation, and the Department of Health, among others.

Despite the multibillion-dollar budget already obligated for the reconstruction, the fact is only $251.7 million have been disbursed so far. That is less than three percent of the obligated funds after more than four years since the disaster.

Still, the COR3 executive characterized 2021 as "the year of transition." and anticipated 2022 to be "the year of construction," with 2,000 permanent projects to go into the bidding process or start construction.

Laboy declined to specify how many of the 2,000 projects he estimated could be under construction by 2022 because "things could happen along the way" that could delay some processes. Nevertheless, he did anticipate the some $3 billion would be disbursed during 2022.

Questioned again about the "lengthy bureaucratic process" projects have to go through at both the federal and state level to be ready for bidding or to begin construction, Laboy reiterated "the foundation for this project" to move forward has already been laid.

Laboy did admit the whole process could take between six to seven months to get approved for bidding, with FEMA taking about three or four months of that time to complete its evaluation. It would then seem a tall order to anticipate 2,000 projects will be ready for bidding or to start construction this next year.

Laboy assured he has been in communication with FEMA and that the federal agency has assured it will revise its procedures to try and cut down the evaluation period. But that is not necessarily guaranteed.

As now processes stand FEMA, the COR3 and all state government agencies taking part in the evaluation of these projects would need to average more than 166 projects a month to reach their 2000 project goal for 2022.

While Laboy assured his office has the capability to deal with 166 projects a month "and more," the fact is that their own "Results versus Priority Goals" charts aside from the emergency projects there are just a few projects under construction and or in the bidding phase and/or permanent project reported as completed, when compared to the total number of projects.

Of the total 1,308 projects obligated in 2020 and 220 obligated this year, COR3 reports a little more than 270 under FEMA's Accelerated Award Strategy, FAAST, and 1,649 under government or not for profit organizations, PNPO, are under architectural and engineering design. The cost of these projects amounts to $3 billion.

Under construction there are only four under FAAST, for a total of only $43 million. Meanwhile 553 projects from government entities and PNPOs are under construction, for a total cost of $373 million.

No FAAST project is reported as completed and only five are under permitting or construction bidding.

Even though funds for 7,000 projects have already been obligated but only a fraction of those are up for bidding, under construction or completed, FEMA's promise to obligate 2,000 in 2022 seems very difficult to fulfill. More so, if you consider that in 2020 the agency manages to obligate 1,308 projects and 220 this year.

This delays in Puerto Rico's recovery process becomes more difficult to understand when the number of obligated housing projects is considered.

According to Laboy, only one housing project, Alturas de Ciales, in Ciales, has been obligated in these four years.

Nevertheless, Laboy assured that a significant number of housing projects will be obligated by the end of next January. He did not specify if any of these projects are included in the 2,000 expected to be up for bidding or under construction in 2022.

Laboy also admitted another area that is "extremely delayed" is the collection and disposal of debris left by hurricane María.

"Unfortunately, there is still a significant amount of trash and debris left by María that hasn't been collected", Laboy said.

The COR3 executive did not anticipated how or when the authorities are going to attend to that situation.

# CHAPTER 28

# Trump's tossing of Paper towels in Puerto Rico

The video clip has played on a repeating loop on cable news this week as Hurricane Florence closed in on the East Coast: President Trump casually tosses rolls of paper towels into a cheering crowd at a church in San Juan, Puerto Rico, after the island was devastated by Hurricane Maria a year ago.

White House aides reacted at the time with a mix of smirks and chuckles over what they saw as classic Trump.

Acting insensitively but, in his own way, playfully to offer amusement to locals who were happy to see him.

A pool reporter that day called the scene "surreal" and described Trump doing his "best Stephen Curry impersonation" as he aimed the towels to the far reaches of the crowd, a performance "they enjoyed."

Nearly a year later, viewed in the prism of a new report about the lethal legacy of Maria, the moment last October does not seem as lighthearted. Trump's day in San Juan limited to the better fortified neighborhoods of the capital and far from the most catastrophic destruction.

This included other scenes that suggested the president was eager to congratulate himself prematurely and to minimize a rapidly deepening tragedy.

The paper-towel moment has come to symbolize what critics say is Trump's inability to sympathize with others and his self-absorbed leadership in a time of crisis.

"One could argue it was nothing but then you could argue it was everything," José Andrés, the celebrity chef who oversaw a massive operation to provide meals on the island, said in an interview Thursday. "It showed such a lack of empathy."

Trump's performance reminds some of a Republican predecessor, George W. Bush, who declared "mission accomplished" in May 2003 during a visit to an aircraft carrier supporting troops in the Iraq War—which would slog on eight more years.

Two years later, Bush rushed to congratulate his Federal Emergency Management Agency director for a "heckuva job" in response to Hurricane Katrina, a storm that was blamed for the deaths of more than 1,800 people.

At the makeshift supply center last October at Calvary Chapel, Trump scoffed at a water purification kit that could help save lives. He awarded "A+" grades for his administration for its response to a pair of other hurricanes that struck Texas, Louisiana, and Florida. And he characterized a death toll of 16 in Puerto Rico as a kind of victory, though the count would officially grow to 34 later in the day.

"There's a lot of love in this room," Trump, wearing a dark hooded windbreaker, boasted in the church.

Things look far grimmer approaching Maria's first anniversary. A report last month from George Washington University, commissioned by the Puerto Rican government, found that an estimated 2,975 more people died on the island in the six months following the storm than would have been expected under typical mortality rates. This was the figure that Puerto Rico's governor accepted as the official death toll.

Trump, furious over what he considers revisionist history, has angrily watched the clips of him tossing paper towels on television and disputed the death numbers Thursday on Twitter, declaring it a conspiracy from the Democrats.

On the island, many residents have homed in on Trump's moment at the church.

"That was disrespectful," said Ramon Pachaco, 58, whose house in Ponce, on the island's southern coast, suffered $26,000 in damage. Trump's message to residents, he said, amounted to: "If you want to cry, dry your tears with this."

Maria wasn't the only crisis the president was dealing with as he and first lady Melania Trump emerged from the White House just after 8 a.m. on Oct. 3, 2017, to start the day trip to San Juan.

Two days earlier, a gunman had slaughtered 58 people at an outdoor country music concert in Las Vegas.

On the South Lawn, the president responded to shouted questions from reporters, calling the mass shooting a "tragedy." Asked about Puerto Rico, Trump declared victory in an escalating battle with San Juan Mayor Carmen Yulín Cruz, who had criticized his administration's response.

"It's now acknowledged what a great job we've done," Trump declared. "In Texas and in Florida, we get an A+. I think we've done just as good in Puerto Rico."

White House aides viewed the president's trip as an important visual counterbalance to his response to the storms on the mainland. Trump already had visited Texas and Florida, but he had appeared more callous toward Puerto Rico, criticizing the island's poor infrastructure, including the electrical grid, and complaining that the cost of the emergency response would throw the federal budget "out of whack."

On June 1, 2018, file photo, a child shines a light on hundreds of shoes at a memorial for those killed by Hurricane Maria in front of the Puerto Rico Capitol in San Juan.

To Mark Merritt, who served as a FEMA manager in the Clinton administration, Trump had already set the wrong tone for his visit.

"No one ever gives themselves a grade on disaster response," said Merritt, who has served as a consultant for the Puerto Rico government over the past year. "The president should have come out and said, 'This is the first truly catastrophic disaster in U.S. history. Never have we had a state that has been devastated with 100 percent of the state impacted."

Aides had set up a full itinerary. The Trumps would meet with people affected by the storm, receive a briefing from local officials and greet U.S. sailors and Marines assisting in the recovery.

"I've been to Puerto Rico many times and the weather is second to none, but sometimes you get hit and you got hit," Trump said, after disembarking Air Force One at a National Guard base in San Juan.

Energy Secretary Rick Perry, who had accompanied Trump, gave Puerto Rico Gov. Ricardo Rosselló a hug and an emphatic handshake. Rosselló, in contrast to the San Juan mayor, had spoken positively of the White House.

After a private briefing, the Trumps proceeded on a walking tour of the relatively affluent Guaynabo neighborhood, where they posed for photos with a local family.

Next stop was Calvary Chapel, for the carefully scripted photo op of Trump handing out supplies. It was something he had done a month earlier in a subdivision in Fort Myers, Fla., where he and the first lady, along with Vice President Pence, had passed out hoagies and bottled water to residents affected by Hurricane Irma.

As soon as Trump entered the church in San Juan, dozens of locals began cheering, snapping photos, and straining to shake his hand.

'It totally belittled the moment'

Andrés was disgusted by Trump's behavior in the church.

"You don't throw them. You hand them," he said of the paper towels. "You look the people in the eye and tell them, 'We're here for you, and we'll do our best to provide relief for you and your family.'"

Current and former White House aides acknowledged that the imagery was unhelpful, overshadowing the breadth of the administration's response. The federal government approved $1.39 billion in grants for more than 462,000 homeowners and renters, and the U.S. Small Business Administration authorized $1.8 billion in low-interest disaster loans, aides said.

"Our sense was that it was a good trip, the president did well, and a lot of the coverage was unfair," said one former administration official, who spoke on anonymity to discuss the thinking of the president's team.

The paper towel moment "was relatively minor and the media exploited it," this person added.

Another former official argued that "the throwing of the paper towels was one of the funniest things of all time" and brought a bit of humor to an otherwise somber visit.

Nearly a year later, White House aides have tried to keep Trump focused on the looming threat of Florence. More than 1.5 million people have been evacuated from coastal regions in the Southeast.

The president has become increasingly infuriated by the focus on his San Juan trip, aides said.

It's a far cry from last October, as Air Force One streaked back from San Juan toward Washington and a triumphant Trump chatted with reporters on the plane.

Asked if he'd received any constructive criticism, the president replied: "None. They were so thankful for what we've done. I think it's been a great day. No, we only heard thank you from the people of Puerto Rico."

# CHAPTER 29

## On Anniversary of Hurricane Maria

Hurricane Fiona flooded Puerto Rico with unrelenting rain and terrifying flash floods on Monday, forcing harrowing home rescues and making it difficult for power crews to reach many parts of the island.

Now the island is once again in darkness, five years after Hurricane Maria inflicted more damage on Puerto Rico than any other disaster in recent history.

While Fiona will be the direct cause, Puerto Ricans will also blame years of power disruptions, the result of an unbearably slow effort to finally give the island a stable control grid.

Hurricane Maria, a near-Category 5 storm, hit on Sept. 20, 2017, leaving about 3,000 dead, and damaging 80 percent of the system. The last house was not reconnected to the system until nearly a year later. Hurricane Fiona, with far less vicious winds, is the strongest storm to reach the island since.

Its plentiful rain, more than 30 inches in some areas in southern Puerto Rico and its central mountainous region, caused the island's huge pattern of canals and creeks to swell, turned entire streets into muddy rivers and forced the rescues of more than 1,000 people.

At least one person died, while operating a generator, while another death was recorded in the Dominican Republic.

"I've never seen this in my life, not even in Maria," said Ada Belmot Plaza, who had to be rescued by the Puerto Rico National Guard as waist-high floodwaters rose outside her daughter's house in the El Coquí neighborhood of Salinas, on Puerto Rico's southern coast.

Some Puerto Ricans said Hurricane Fiona took them by surprise, and many in the hardest-hit areas were still waiting for government help as neighbors came together to clear fallen trees from roads and remove rubble from homes.

Gov. Pedro R. Pierluisi urged people to stay indoors. He said he expected most electricity to be back up "in a matter of days." By Monday morning, power had been restored to some 100,000 customers, out of 1.5 million.

The federal government paid $3.2 billion to patch up the island's electrical grid in Hurricane Maria's wake. But that was just to get the power back on; Congress earmarked an additional $10 billion to modernize the antiquated and inefficient system.

The Puerto Rico government and the fiscal board appointed by Congress to oversee the island's finances required that the power transmission and distribution system be privatized after thinking the Puerto Rico Electric Power Authority, which is bankrupt but continues to run power generation, to be ineffective.

Funds from the Federal Emergency Management Agency will finance any new upgrades.

In 2020, Puerto Rico awarded a 15-year contract to LUMA Energy, a private Canadian American consortium, for a fixed annual fee of $115 million.

After taking over in June of last year, the company quickly struggled with rolling summer blackouts. There was an island wide outage in April, with no bad weather in sight.

In the wake of Hurricane Fiona, most Puerto Ricans face the overwhelming prospect of spoiled food and medication, sticky nights and the other familiar risks and indignities of being plunged into darkness.

They are somewhat better equipped this time because those who could afford generators bought them after the Hurricane Maria fiasco. That came with its own dangers: Officials on Monday said a man died while trying to operate a generator. His wife suffered severe burns but survived.

In the Dominican Republic, the storm killed at least one person, a 68-year-old man who was hit by a falling tree in the northern province of María Trinidad Sánchez, according to local media.

As Hurricane Fiona moved westward, it battered the eastern provinces of the Dominican Republic, home to one of the largest tourism industries in the Caribbean.

Heavy rain and 90-mile-per-hour winds set off mudslides that shuttered resorts and damaged highways, officials said.

The storm is expected to pass near the islands of Turks and Caicos on Tuesday before strengthening at sea into a major hurricane, a Category 3 or higher, by Wednesday, the National Hurricane Center said. It is not forecast to approach the East Coast of the United States.

In Puerto Rico, overflowing waterways and the loss of power caused pumps to fail, leaving 70 percent of households and businesses that rely on the public water and sewer system without potable water.

Governor Pierluisi said he had been coordinating with the White House to receive assistance. President Biden issued an emergency declaration on Sunday, unlocking federal funding and FEMA support.

President Biden called Governor Pierluisi from Air Force One as the president returned from of Queen Elizabeth's funeral II in London, according to the White House.

The States also lined up to send mutual aid. New York said more than 100 Spanish-speaking members of the State Police would help clear streets, direct traffic, and respond to other needs in Puerto Rico.

Most customers who had electricity on Monday, including a couple of hospitals, were in the San Juan metropolitan area, which was spared the worst of Hurricane Fiona's rains.

The damage from Fiona's floodwaters is expected to be enormous, in the "billions," Governor Pierluisi estimated. A sobering reminder that a storm's categorization under the Saffir-Simpson scale considers its maximum wind speeds, but not its rainfall or storm surge potential.

In the town of Cayey, residents had to clear out the mud after the La Plata River surged and almost completely submerged a two-story house. A temporary bridge erected over the Guaonica River in Utuado buckled, its demise captured on dramatic video as rushing waters and debris washed it away.

The bridge was put up after Hurricane Maria to connect devastated neighborhoods in the area, and a new, permanent bridge was scheduled to go up in 2024.

In Santa Isabel, on the southern coast of the island, Itzamary Alvarado said she had more water in her house than during Hurricane Maria. Government officials, she said, should have given the public more warning about Hurricane Fiona, which had initially approached the island as a tropical storm.

"I think the government minimized what was going to happen," Ms. Alvarado said. "I found out it was a hurricane at 11 a.m. on Sunday, so I left everything and ran to the supermarket. I had not prepared for a hurricane."

For her and many others, the storm was a test of whether the government response to disasters would be better after Maria.

"We have been struggling for five years and see the same conditions from the government in the management of emergency situations," Ms. Alvarado said. "It's frustrating."

She suddenly had a sign that things were changing for the better: Trucks from Puerto Rico's power company, LUMA, appeared on her street.

"A LUMA brigade just drove by my house," she said. "I've never seen that before."

Comparisons to Hurricane Maria were inevitable, from both residents and officials.

The island's hospitals were running on backup generators, in stark contrast to 2017, when many lost powers, damaging medical equipment and leaving hundreds of sick patients dangerously at risk.

About 75 percent of cellphone towers were still functioning after the storm passed, compared with the near-total signal wipeout five years ago.

Governor Pierluisi stressed that officials were still in the rescue-and-response phase of the emergency and had not begun to assess the scale of the damage or determine the island's path to recovery. Still, he said, the local government's response had so far been "exemplary" compared with what happened after Maria.

"Maria served as a lesson, an exercise for our emergency response teams at all levels," Governor Pierluisi, a member of the pro-statehood New Progressive Party who took office in 2021, said in a news conference. "In terms of the coordination we've seen, there's a big difference."

Hurricane Maria, which struck within weeks of Hurricane Irma in 2017, laid bare the fragile state of the island's aging, poorly maintained infrastructure.

Its powerful winds, with gusts exceeding 100 m.p.h., destroyed thousands of homes, and wiped out the island's agriculture and access to communications. Recovery was painfully sluggish, and the lack of potable water, fuel, and food supplies in the wake of the storm prompted an exodus of tens of thousands of residents to the United States mainland.

Public fury bubbled up at the government's response to the storm. In 2019, a grass-roots movement channeling the anger formed, fueling a popular uprising in 2019 that lasted 15 days and caused former Gov. Ricardo A. Rosselló to step down.

Puerto Ricans remain unconvinced of their leaders' abilities to respond to disasters.

In Salinas on Monday, Ana Medina Cardona, 74, said government reconstruction contractors had repaired a section of her tin roof that was torn apart by Hurricane Maria.

On Sunday, rain started pouring through that repaired roof while she was home with her dog, Famy.

"It seems they didn't do a great job, because water was coming down the walls," Ms. Medina Cardona said. "This time around, it was even worse than in Maria."

She waited in a shelter to hear if the water had receded enough for her to return home. But she was unconvinced it was her best option.

"If we can go back," she said, "that also means going back there to a house without power."

# CHAPTER 30

# Hurricane Fiona Continue

Hurricane Fiona continues to head north Wednesday away from the Turks and Caicos and has intensified into a Category 4 hurricane in the southwestern Atlantic.

The powerful storm could strengthen even further as it tracks toward Bermuda over the next two days, prompting the issuance of a Hurricane Watch for the British island territory.

Fiona battered the Turks and Caicos on Tuesday as high winds and heavy rain spread across the islands after the hurricane had already turned deadly in Puerto Rico and the Dominican Republic.

Fiona made two landfalls as a Category 1 hurricane, the first one Sunday afternoon along the extreme southwestern coast of Puerto Rico and the second one early Monday morning in the eastern Dominican Republic.

In Puerto Rico, the city of Ponce clocked a 103-mph wind gust, while in the Dominican Republic, a gust of 98 mph was recorded in Samana at El Catey International Airport.

The high winds plunged all of Puerto Rico into a blackout on Sunday as catastrophic flooding unfolded across the U.S. territory.

# CHAPTER 31

## Puerto Rico has been devastated by Hurricane Fiona.

The island received the heaviest rainfall recorded in 123 years, more than 25 municipalities were severely flooded, and hundreds of residents lost their homes and belongings.

In the following, you will read about different situation around the island. I just moved from Ponce to Mayaguez. I suffered a lot during Maria.

This time, I was far from the southern part of Puerto Rico. I was lucky...

### Leida Rodriguez tell her story.

When Leida Rodriguez started building a house in <u>Villa Esperanza</u>, neighbors suggested she lift it because the nearby Rio Nigua rose a few feet during Hurricane Maria nothing these weathered coastal souls hadn't seen before.

She built the house four feet off the ground, hoping to lessen coastal flooding in southern Puerto Rico, where she found an affordable spot in a beautiful community to live out her retirement.

She never imagined that a <u>Category-1 cyclone</u> would bring so much rain that the beams of her white-and-blue trim home would buckle and slide into a deep mud hole.

"It was my refuge, my place of peace," said Rodriguez, 50, who along with her husband used their life savings to build the home blocked by concrete.

"We thought it wasn't going to happen. No one had ever seen flooding like what happened."

Hurricane Fiona dumped at least half as much rain as the coastal town of Salinas, where most residents live in flood zones. Though the storm brought far less powerful winds than Category-4 Maria in 2017, some parts of the main island experienced just as much rain or more.

Many were caught off guard. First responders rescued hundreds of people from flooded homes and some roads and bridges repaired after Maria were destroyed again.

The U.S. government made historic allocations, including more than $3 billion for hazard mitigation, to Puerto Rico after Maria, some of which was scheduled to go toward preventing severe flooding during storms.

A separate pot of federal public assistance money is designated for rebuilding public infrastructure.

In Salinas, which was smacked by Maria and battered again by Fiona, officials have submitted 74 projects to the Federal Emergency Management Agency for funding.

To date, just seven, including road repairs and a basketball court, have been completed, according to data from Puerto Rico's Central Office for Recovery, Reconstruction and Resiliency. About two dozen more entered the construction phase in the last six months.

Salinas officials have identified 44 potential justification projects. So far, they've submitted three, including a proposal to build a water treatment plant that was approved in December and is in the design phase.

Two other projects under review propose installing generators at critical facilities and a new storm water system on public streets leading to a hospital. Neither one of those projects has been constructed.

"I'm pretty sure if these extenuation plans would have been carried out, it would've mitigated the issues that some of these municipalities experienced," said researcher Jennifer Hinojosa, who works for Hunter

College's Center for Puerto Rican Studies in New York and been tracking the recovery from Maria.

Instead, residents and experts say unrestrained coastal construction, mangrove destruction, deforestation, coastal erosion, and poor canal maintenance have heightened the risk for marginalized communities like Salinas, a town of 25,000.

Across the island archipelago, 5 percent of the available post-Maria FEMA funds for hazard mitigation have been obligated, according to the data from Puerto Rico's recovery office, a first hurdle in getting a project started. The cumbersome management of those funds at both the federal and local level is slowing down Puerto Rico's slow long-term resiliency reconstruction, experts said.

FEMA officials said they are continuing to work with municipalities to help stave off the most severe—and in some cases, preventable— damage when a storm rolls through.

"Hurricanes are a natural phenomenon," said Victor Alvarado, a local environmental activist. "Disasters are man-made."

## 'Maria didn't do this'

Puerto Rico's southern region is drier than its northern coast, and its topography makes it prone to rapid flooding. Hurricane Fiona concentrated its heavy rainfall over the southern slopes of the central mountains where water rushes down steep highlands and spills into the coastal plain until it reaches the sea.

The soil is often unable to absorb all the moisture, and instead it runs off the surface, according to meteorologists and regional climatological reports.

While the eye of the storm swirled westward, it dragged a line of intense weather that brought with it sustained humidity. That system pounded the southern coast with relentless precipitation.

"It's a double whammy. You have a hurricane with strong gusts and then a tail of intense rain that remained stationary over the south dropping two to three feet of water," said University of Wisconsin meteorologist Ángel Adames-Corraliza, a native of Puerto Rico. "That's a nightmare scenario."

Weeks earlier, Salinas residents had been worried about persistent drought conditions threatening their aquifer and only source of drinking water in the municipality.

Today, many neighbors are struggling to understand why the flood was so fierce that it triggered midnight rescues for hundreds who said they had never seen so much water. Engorged streams and creeks burst in all directions. The Rio Nigua jumped its banks and discharged into channels never carved in recent memory.

Daniel and Maria, De Jesús have lived confidently inside their home in the Coquí community of Salinas for more than 40 years, never experiencing a severe deluge. The house sits a few feet above the low-lying roadway. Yet several hours into Fiona's downpours, brackish water invaded their bedroom.

"I've never felt so much fear," said Daniel De Jesús, 76, whose family was rescued by National Guard troops Sunday. "I stayed here during Maria. If I had done the same for Fiona, I would not be here to talk about it."

Pieces of newly laid runway was shattered like fragments of glass and scattered about the neighborhood. The smell of rot was unavoidable as residents piled their waterlogged furniture on the curb next to mounds of riverbed soil and sheared vegetation.

Families wound out their clothes hoping the blistering post-storm sun would dry them out and get rid of the unmistakable odor of mold.

The De Jesús family lost most of their possessions. But that is not what worries them. They said they have warily watched how new construction projects, such as a nearby solar farm and housing developments, have taken little care for the geography and risks of the flood plain.

"Nature is reclaiming and telling us this belongs to her," Daniel De Jesús said. "As the saying goes, the river always finds its course."

Developers build too close to creeks and canals. They compact the soil and fill in wetlands with sand and gravel. They change natural water flows, said environmental lawyer Ruth Santiago, who works closely with a coalition of community-based organizations.

"There are things that are being approved...that are making the flooding worse," she said.

Salinas Mayor Karilyn Bonilla Colón did not respond to interview requests but has been vocal in the local press about using the federal dollars principally for flood mitigation and urban renewal.

Illegal coastal construction in protected estuaries and sensitive land reserves, such as nearby Jobos Bay, has become a flash point for locals and other Puerto Ricans living near the ocean. In recent years, communities have waged court battles and protested the central government giving what they see as illegal permits to builders destroying mangrove forests and exacerbating flooding.

Mangroves act as natural barriers that protect communities from storm surge and can absorb water, among other ecological benefits. These same communities saw flood levels rise dangerously in the middle of the night, Santiago said.

"Puerto Rico is a group of islands that is very limited in geographic space. It can be described as a mountain range surrounded by a narrow coastal plain. And that coastal plain is very narrow in the south," Santiago said. "So, you can't keep building, using up land space. Floodwaters need areas that are not impacted by construction to go out to the sea without causing damage."

Victor Bonilla said he held out if he could but when the water reached nearly a foot in height at 12:30 a.m. on Monday, he put his two boys and wife inside a dump truck that was helping to evacuate residents of barrio Playita—walking distance from the popular Punta Arenas beach.

"I didn't want to leave. I'm a fighter but when you have a family, you've got to surrender," said Bonilla, 37, whose family has lived and fished here for generations. "You learn how to live with flooding and adjust but we didn't think this storm would do this. Maria didn't do this."

The type of construction work that should be happening, residents and experts say, has not transpired in decades. Levees, canal dredging, sea walls and other diversions are the kind of flood control measures the U.S. Army Corps of Engineers has long studied in this region. They've made recommendations and drawn up detailed plans, but the work either was not funded or was not completed, local officials and residents said.

In 2018, Puerto Rico's congressional representative, Jenniffer González Colón(R), announced the approval of $2.5 billion of federal funding for flood control projects, including the canalization and construction of levees along Rio Nigua in Salinas. Some work has begun and is in the design phase, but not in time to make a difference for hundreds of families like the ones community leader Ismenia Figueroa serves.

"You learn to fight for what's yours here and depend on no one," said Figueroa, 60, her eyes reddening with tears. "But the sense of powerlessness can be so suffocating."

This is the kind of thing Puerto Ricans in these Salinas neighborhoods and leaders said they have come to expect: Many overtures and announcements but lagging progress.

The sluggish pace of FEMA dollars reaching those communities with the most urgent infrastructure needs is a frustrating fact of life for residents. Much of the completed public infrastructure work in Puerto Rico has gone to rehabbing roads or rebuilding recreational facilities, records show, after Hurricane Maria.

The work is necessary, community leaders say, but so many of the projects that require significant investment, engineering, and design to create resiliency stay suspended in the proposal phase. Some of these plans and requests for hazard mitigation date back to declared disasters from previous hurricanes, according to FEMA data obtained by The Washington Post.

The delays are the consequence of bureaucratic hurdles and management struggles at the state and federal level, said former FEMA hazard mitigation expert and historian, Rafael Torrech. The veteran grant writer was brought in after Hurricane Maria to help guide applicants through the process. Hazard mitigation projects normally take longer and can take a back seat to the rebuilding of public infrastructure because they are focused on planning for the future.

FEMA has dedicated staff, but the mechanisms for releasing money are outdated and ill-suited to long-term reconstruction, Torrech said. The added complications of Puerto Rico's bankruptcy and lack of access to financing meant the government could not afford to put out bids for work through the federal agency's reimbursement model. It took time for FEMA, Puerto Rico's recovery office and the fiscal oversight board managing the commonwealth's finances to develop cash flow solutions.

By then, there were labor and material shortages driven by the pandemic, transportation issues and an ongoing exodus from Puerto Rico. A limited supply of professional firms able to do design and engineering work from the island archipelago drove up costs.

"Puerto Rico is a perfect example of everything that went wrong," Torrech said. "Practically, none of the mitigation projects has gotten to the construction phase. You cannot control nature, but you can control your reaction to it. It's a question of management."

It's a cycle that has been repeated disaster after disaster, experts said. Soon, the only options left for some of Puerto Rico's most under-resourced communities such as those in Salinas, is to abandon their homes and relocate.

Wanda Lee considered it. The 44-year-old left her seaside home to start anew in Pennsylvania, overwhelmed by the weeks of powerlessness and joblessness in the aftermath of Maria. But, she said, the island called her back home.

Then came Fiona. Lee was asleep for most of it, relegating the storm to an afterthought. When she awoke and stood up from her bed, she stepped into a puddle of water. The flooding was worse than five years earlier and she and her neighbors had to be rescued from their homes. But this time, she won't be packing up.

"I stick out the storms and I stick out these hurricanes because it's part of me," Lee said in front of her newly waterlogged home. "I'm a playera," or beach lover, "and this is what we do."

Rodriguez, the woman who lost her house to a mudslide near the river, spent hours on the phone Thursday with federal officials to see if she qualifies for help. She said she is not optimistic because the low-cost lot where her house once stood was in a flood zone where many of her neighbors did not get help after Maria.

"I will recover," she said. "But I won't rebuild here."

# CHAPTER 32

## Hurricane Ian strikes Cuba

Hurricane Ian tore into western Cuba as a major hurricane Tuesday, knocking out power to the entire country and leaving 11 million people without electricity, before churning on a collision course with Florida over warm Gulf waters amid expectations it would strengthen into a catastrophic Category 4 storm.

Ian made landfall in Cuba's Pinar del Rio province, where officials set up 55 shelters, evacuated 50,000 people, and took steps to protect crops in the nation's main tobacco-growing region. The U.S. National Hurricane Center said Cuba suffered "significant wind and storm surge impacts" when the hurricane struck with top sustained winds of 125 mph (205 kmh).

Ian was expected to get even stronger over the warm Gulf of Mexico, reaching top winds of 130 mph (209 kph) approaching the southwest coast of Florida, where 2.5 million people were ordered to evacuate.

Tropical storm-force winds were expected across the southern peninsula late Tuesday, reaching hurricane-force Wednesday—when the eye was predicted to make landfall. With tropical storm-force winds extending 140 miles (225 kilometers) from Ian's center, damage was expected across a wide area of Florida.

It was not yet clear precisely where Ian would crash ashore. Its exact track could determine how severe the storm surge is for Tampa Bay, said University of Miami hurricane researcher Brian McNoldy. Landfall south of the bay could make the impact "much less bad," McNoldy said.

Gil Gonzalez boarded up his windows Tuesday and had sandbags ready to protect his Tampa home. He and his wife had stocked up on bottled water and packed flashlights, battery packs for their cellphones and a camp stove before evacuating.

"All the prized possessions, we've put them upstairs in a friend's house and nearby, and we've got the car loaded," Gonzalez said on his way out.

Florida Gov. Ron DeSantis urged people to prepare for extended power outages, and to get out of the storm's potential path.

"It is a big storm, it is going to kick up a lot of water as it comes in," DeSantis told a news conference in Sarasota, a coastal city of 57,000 that could be hit. "And you're going to end up with significant storm surge and you're going to end up with significant flood events. And this is the kind of storm surge that is life threatening."

He said about 30,000 utility workers have already been positioned around the state, but it might take days before they can safely reach some of the downed power lines.

"This thing's the real deal," DeSantis said. "It is a major, major storm."

DeSantis said nearly 100 shelters had been opened by Tuesday afternoon, with more expected. He said most buildings in Florida are strong enough to withstand wind, but the 2.5 million people who have been told to evacuate face the greatest danger from flooding.

Hundreds of residents were being evacuated from several nursing homes in the Tampa area, where hospitals were also moving some patients. Airports in Tampa, St. Petersburg and Key West closed. Busch Gardens in Tampa closed ahead of the storm, while several Orlando-area theme parks, including Disney World and Sea World, planned to close Wednesday and Thursday.

NASA rolled its moon rocket from the launch pad to its Kennedy Space Center hangar, adding weeks of delay to the test flight.

Ian's forward movement was expected to slow over the Gulf, enabling the hurricane to grow wider and stronger. The hurricane warning expanded Tuesday to cover roughly 220 miles (350 kilometers) of Florida's west coast. The area includes Fort Myers as well as Tampa and

St. Petersburg, which could get their first direct hit by a major hurricane since 1921.

Forecasters said the storm surge could reach 12 feet (3.6 meters) if it peaks at high tide. Rainfall near the area of landfall could top 18 inches (46 centimeters). They also reported a threat of isolated tornados being kicked up by the storm's approach across Florida.

"It's a monster and then there's the confusion of the path," said Renee Correa, who headed inland to Orlando from the Tampa area with her daughter and Chihuahua. "Tampa has been lucky for 100 years, but it's a little scary now."

Kelly Johnson was preparing to hunker down at her home two blocks from the beach in Dunedin, west of Tampa. She said she would escape to the second floor if sea water surges inland, and had a generator if power goes out.

"I'm a Floridian, and we know how to deal with hurricanes," Johnson said. "This is part of living in paradise—knowing that once in a while these storms come at you."

Forecasters warned the hurricane will be felt across a large area as it plows across Florida with an anticipated turn northward. Flash floods were possible across the whole state, and portions of Florida's east coast faced a potential storm surge threat as Ian's bands approach the Atlantic Ocean. Parts of Georgia and South Carolina also could see flooding rains into the weekend.

Georgia Gov. Brian Kemp pre-emptively declared a state of emergency Tuesday, ordering 500 National Guard troops on standby to respond as needed.

As the storm's center moved into the Gulf, scenes of destruction emerged in Cuba's world-famous tobacco belt. The owner of the premier Finca Robaina cigar producer posted photos on social media of wood-and-thatch roofs smashed to the ground, greenhouses in rubble and wagons overturned.

"It was apocalyptic, a real disaster," wrote Hirochi Robaina, grandson of the operation's founder.

Local government station TelePinar reported heavy damage at the main hospital in Pinar del Rio city, tweeting photos of collapsed ceilings and toppled trees. No deaths were reported.

Hurricane Ian tore into western Cuba as a major hurricane Tuesday, knocking out power to the entire country and leaving 11 million people without electricity, before churning on a collision course with Florida over warm Gulf waters amid expectations it would strengthen into a catastrophic Category 4 storm.

Ian made landfall in Cuba's Pinar del Rio province, where officials set up 55 shelters, evacuated 50,000 people, and took steps to protect crops in the nation's main tobacco-growing region. The U.S. National Hurricane Center said Cuba suffered "significant wind and storm surge impacts" when the hurricane struck with top sustained winds of 125 mph (205 kmh).

Ian was expected to get even stronger over the warm Gulf of Mexico, reaching top winds of 130 mph (209 kph) approaching the southwest coast of Florida, where 2.5 million people were ordered to evacuate.

Tropical storm-force winds were expected across the southern peninsula late Tuesday, reaching hurricane-force Wednesday, when the eye was predicted to make landfall. With tropical storm-force winds extending 140 miles (225 kilometers) from Ian's center, damage was expected across a wide area of Florida.

It was not yet clear precisely where Ian would crash ashore. Its exact track could determine how severe the storm surge is for Tampa Bay, said University of Miami hurricane researcher Brian McNoldy. Landfall south of the bay could make the impact "much less bad," McNoldy said.

Gil Gonzalez boarded up his windows Tuesday and had sandbags ready to protect his Tampa home. He and his wife had stocked up on bottled water and packed flashlights, battery packs for their cellphones and a camp stove before evacuating.

"All the prized possessions, we've put them upstairs in a friend's house and nearby, and we've got the car loaded," Gonzalez said on his way out.

Florida Gov. Ron DeSantis urged people to prepare for extended power outages, and to get out of the storm's potential path.

"It is a big storm, it is going to kick up a lot of water as it comes in," DeSantis told a news conference in Sarasota, a coastal city of 57,000 that could be hit. "And you're going to end up with significant storm surge and you're going to end up with significant flood events. And this is the kind of storm surge that is life threatening."

He said about 30,000 utility workers have already been positioned around the state, but it might take days before they can safely reach some of the downed power lines.

"This thing's the real deal," DeSantis said. "It is a major, major storm."

DeSantis said nearly 100 shelters had been opened by Tuesday afternoon, with more expected. He said most buildings in Florida are strong enough to withstand wind, but the 2.5 million people who have been told to evacuate face the greatest danger from flooding.

Hundreds of residents were being evacuated from several nursing homes in the Tampa area, where hospitals were also moving some patients. Airports in Tampa, St. Petersburg and Key West closed. Busch Gardens in Tampa closed ahead of the storm, while several Orlando-area theme parks, including Disney World and Sea World, planned to close Wednesday and Thursday.

NASA rolled its moon rocket from the launch pad to its Kennedy Space Center hangar, adding weeks of delay to the test flight.

Ian's forward movement was expected to slow over the Gulf, enabling the hurricane to grow wider and stronger. The hurricane warning expanded Tuesday to cover roughly 220 miles (350 kilometers) of Florida's west coast. The area includes Fort Myers as well as Tampa and St. Petersburg, which could get their first direct hit by a major hurricane since 1921.

Forecasters said the storm surge could reach 12 feet (3.6 meters) if it peaks at high tide. Rainfall near the area of landfall could top 18 inches, 46 centimeters. They also reported a threat of isolated tornados being kicked up by the storm's approach across Florida.

"It's a monster and then there's the confusion of the path," said Renee Correa, who headed inland to Orlando from the Tampa area with her daughter and Chihuahua. "Tampa has been lucky for 100 years, but it's a little scary now."

Kelly Johnson was preparing to hunker down at her home two blocks from the beach in Dunedin, west of Tampa. She said she would escape to the second floor if sea water surges inland, and had a generator if power goes out.

"I'm a Floridian, and we know how to deal with hurricanes," Johnson said. "This is part of living in paradise, knowing that once in a while these storms come at you."

Forecasters warned the hurricane will be felt across a large area as it plows across Florida with an anticipated turn northward. Flash floods were possible across the whole state, and portions of Florida's east coast faced a potential storm surge threat as Ian's bands approach the Atlantic Ocean. Parts of Georgia and South Carolina also could see flooding rains into the weekend.

Georgia Gov. Brian Kemp pre-emptively declared a state of emergency Tuesday, ordering 500 National Guard troops on standby to respond as needed.

As the storm's center moved into the Gulf, scenes of destruction emerged in Cuba's world-famous tobacco belt. The owner of the premier Finca Robaina cigar producer posted photos on social media of wood-and-thatch roofs smashed to the ground, greenhouses in rubble and wagons overturned.

"It was apocalyptic, a real disaster," wrote Hirochi Robaina, grandson of the operation's founder.

Local government station TelePinar reported heavy damage at the main hospital in Pinar del Rio city, tweeting photos of collapsed ceilings and toppled trees. No deaths were reported.

At the White House, President Joe Biden said his administration was sending hundreds of Federal Emergency Management Agency employees to Florida and sought to assure mayors in the storm's path that Washington will meet their needs. He urged residents to heed local officials' orders.

"Your safety is more important than anything," he said.

White House press secretary Karine Jean-Pierre said Biden spoke later Tuesday evening with DeSantis on federal steps to help Florida prepare for the storm and both committed to close coordination.

Anderson reported from St. Petersburg, Florida. Associated Press contributors include Cody Jackson in Tampa, Florida, Freida Frisaro in Miami, Anthony Izaguirre in Tallahassee, Florida, Mike Schneider in

Orlando, Florida, Seung Min Kim and Seth Borenstein in Washington and Bobby Caina Calvan and Julie Walker in New York.

# CHAPTER 33

## Hurricane Ian is Weakening

Hurricane Ian is currently a weakening tropical storm that is impacting the Florida Peninsula having struck the Cayman Islands and western Cuba.

It is the ninth named storm, fourth hurricane, and second major hurricane of the 2022 Atlantic hurricane season.

Ian originated from a tropical wave that was located by the National Hurricane Center east of the Windward Islands on September 19, 2022.

Two days later, the wave moved into the Caribbean Sea, where it brought winds and heavy rain to the ABC islands, Trinidad and Tobago, and the northern coasts of Venezuela and Colombia on September 21–22.

It showed signs of development into a tropical depression later that day, as convection increased and became more focused. After strengthening into Tropical Storm Ian, it became a hurricane as it neared the Cayman Islands, before rapidly intensifying to a high-end Category 3 hurricane as it made landfall in western Cuba.

Significant storm surge and heavy rainfall affected Cuba and the entire province of Pinar del Río lost power. It slightly weakened over land but restrengthened once it moved into the southeastern Gulf of Mexico, becoming a high-end Category 4 hurricane early on September 28, 2022, as it progressed towards the west coast of Florida. Ian weakened slightly as it approached the coast but remained at Category 4 strength as it made two landfalls in Southwest Florida.

So far, two fatalities have occurred with the hurricane, both in Pinar del Río, Cuba.

Additionally, 19 people are missing after a Cuban boat sank because of the hurricane. Recovery efforts are ongoing, but they have not been found.

On September 19, the NHC began tracking a tropical wave (designated as Invest to the east of the Windward Islands for possible gradual development.

Two days later, the disturbance passed over Trinidad and Tobago as it entered the southeast Caribbean, and then near to the ABC Islands and to the northern coast of South America on September 22.

During the same day, as the disturbance tracked west northwestward it showed signs of increasing organization. Strong wind shear of 30–35 mph (45–55 km/h) generated by the upper-level outflow from Hurricane Fiona was, however preventing development into a tropical depression. A well-defined circulation was still able to form within the disturbance the same day; its convection then increased and became persistent overnight into the next day. The result was it was designated Tropical Depression Nine early in the morning on September 23, 2022.

On September 24, 2022, the depression's wind speed had increased to 40 mph (65 km/h), and thus was given the name Ian. At approximately 08:30 UTC on September 27, a rapidly intensifying Ian made landfall on western Cuba with sustained winds of 125 mph (205 km/h), becoming the strongest tropical cyclone to impact Pinar del Río Province since Hurricane Gustav in 2008.

Ian weakened some over land but remained a major hurricane as it emerged off the coast of Cuba and into the southeastern Gulf of Mexico Ian strengthened slightly upon moving offshore, but then initiated an eyewall replacement cycle, causing its wind speed to remain steady at 120 mph, although its pressure continued to fall as the hurricane grew.

It moved over the Dry Tortugas with the same wind speed and a pressure of 947 mb as it continued to reorganize.

After completing the eyewall cycle a few hours later, Ian quickly strengthened, reaching Category 4 intensity on September 28. 2022.

By September 28, 2022, Ian strengthened further to 155 mph (250 km/h) as it neared Southwest Florida, despite outflow being restricted in its southwestern quadrant by moderate wind shear.

Ian made landfall on <u>Cayo Costa</u> with sustained winds of 150 mph (240 km/h) and an estimated central pressure of 940 mb (28 inHg), becoming the first Category 4 hurricane to impact Southwest Florida since Charley in 2004, which also made landfall at the same location.

Ian then made a second landfall just south of <u>Punta Gorda</u> near Pirate Harbor with 145 mph (235 km/h) winds.

Ian weakened to Category 3 ....

## Jamaica

The Meteorological Service of Jamaica issued tropical storm watches for the island of Jamaica on Friday, September 23, 2022. Flood warnings and marine warnings were issued simultaneously.

## Cayman Islands

The government of the Cayman Islands issued hurricane watches for its three islands.

1. Grand Cayman
2. Cayman Brac
3. Little Cayman

On September 23, Ian was projected to pass over the British Overseas Territory as a hurricane.

The National Emergency Operations Centre had gone into full activation mode. Along with the emergency services, the Cayman Islands Regiment and Cayman Islands Coast Guard saw the full mobilization and deployments of their personnel.

In addition, the Governor of the Cayman Islands, Martyn Roper, requested for the United Kingdom to further deploy additional military assets to the islands for the Humanitarian Aid and Disaster Relief (HADR) Operations. Subsequently HMS Medway was deployed to the Cayman Islands. Helicopters from Royal Cayman Islands Police Service were also deployed to assist in the operation.

At the time one of the helicopters was deployed to the <u>Turks and Caicos</u> Islands prior to the development of Ian to assist recovery efforts there after the passage of Hurricane Fiona.

The Royal Navy also deployed its helicopter to assist. Schools, universities, and education centers closed the evening of September 23.

On September 24, 2022, the hurricane watch for Grand Cayman was upgraded to a hurricane warning and the hurricane watch for <u>Cayman Brac</u> and <u>Little Cayman</u> was changed to a tropical storm watch.

Flood warnings along with marine warnings were also issued for Grand Cayman. The Cayman Islands Airports Authority were to continue to operate the airports until the afternoon of September 25, by which the airports would close and all the aircraft at the airports were to be evacuated out.

## Cuba

Authorities in Cuba issued evacuation orders for around 50,000 people in the Pinar del Rio province and set up around 55 shelters prior to the storm.

State media also stated that steps were being taken to protect food and crops in warehouses. Locals removed fishing boats in Havana and city workers inspected and unclogged storm drains.

## United States

Amtrak suspended its Auto Train service for September 27–28 and truncated the September 26 southbound Silver Star at Jacksonville, Florida, on September 27.

Silver Star service was cancelled for September 27–28 with the northbound Silver Star for September 29 also cancelled.

The ninth public hearing of the United States House Select Committee on the January 6 Attack, scheduled for September 28 was postponed.

The governors of North Carolina, South Carolina, and Virginia all declared a state of emergency in preparation of the incoming storm.

## Florida

On September 24, Governor Ron DeSantis declared a state of emergency for the entire state of Florida.

Tampa Bay area schools also announced closures, and several colleges and universities, including the University of South Florida, the University of Tampa, and Eckerd College announced that they were cancelling classes and closing.

By September 27, 2022, 55 public school districts across the state announced cancellations, many through the end of the week. The Artemis 1 launch was delayed due to the storm.

President Joe Biden approved a state of emergency declaration for Florida on September 24, 2022.

Additionally, the Biden Administration declared a public health emergency for Florida as well.

Numerous airports and ports, including in Tampa, Tampa Bay, Orlando, St. Petersburg, and Key West announced that they would be suspending operations.

Walt Disney World and Universal Orlando stated that they would be closing attractions. Numerous stores, including Walmart and Waffle House, were closed because of the impending dangerous weather.

Mandatory evacuation orders were issued for parts of multiple counties.

About 300,000 people may be evacuated from areas of Hillsborough County with schools and other locations being used as shelters. Governor DeSantis mobilized 5,000 Florida state national guard troops with another 2,000 on standby in neighboring states.

Officials in Tallahassee and nearby cities removed rubble and monitored the cities power lines and storm-water systems to make sure the infrastructure systems were prepared and secure. The college football game between the East Carolina Pirates and the South Florida Bulls was moved from South Florida's stadium in Tampa to Boca Raton.

The Tampa Bay Buccaneers of the National Football League moved practices from Tampa south to the Miami Dolphins' training facility in Miami Gardens.

## Georgia

Governor Brian Kemp ordered the activation of the State Operations Center on September 26 to begin preparations for the impact of the storm in the later part of the week. Many farmers prepared prior to the storm by turning off irrigation systems to attempt to dry out the ground and harvest what they could, as much of the state's cotton crop has not been harvested yet. Atlanta Motor Speedway opened their campgrounds to hurricane evacuees.

## South Carolina

The college football game between the South Carolina State Bulldogs and South Carolina Gamecocks scheduled for October 1 at 12:00 p.m. was moved up to September 29 at 7:00 p.m. on account of the storm.

## Bahamas

The eastward shift in Ian's track as well as increasing size of the hurricane prompted the issuance of a tropical storm warning for Bimini and Grand Bahama in The Bahamas late on September 27, 2022.

## Caribbean Cayman Islands

Minimal impacts were felt on the Cayman Islands as the storm passed to its west. The all clear for the Islands was called at 3:00 p.m. EDT on September 26, 2022, from the National Emergency Operations Center.

A couple of inches of rain and wind gusts of up to 50 mph (80 km/h) was observed at Seven Mile Beach on Grand Cayman along with some minor storm surge flooding. Minor damage and scattered power outages were also reported.

## Cuba

Striking western Cuba as a Category 3 hurricane, Ian caused extensive damage throughout Pinar del Río and Mayabeque provinces. The storm made landfall at 4:30 ET on September 27, 2022 in Pinar del Río province.

A peak wind gust of 129 mph (208 km/h) was observed in San Juan y Martínez. A 24-hour rainfall total of 4.26 in (108.3 mm) was measured on Isla de la Juventud. Significant storm surge inundation occurred along the coasts of the Gulf of Guanahacabibes and Isla de la Juventud.

Ian caused a power outage in the province of Pinar del Río, cutting power to the entire province, which had a population of 850,000.[The Cuba Institute of Meteorology located in Havana reported a sustained wind of 56 mph (90 km/h) with a gust to 87 mph (140 km/h) during the afternoon of September 27.[64] Two people were killed in Cuba, a man in San Juan y Martínez who was electrocuted while disconnecting a wind turbine used for irrigating his field, and a 43-year-old woman who died when one of the walls of her house collapsed.

In the early morning of September 28, the storm knocked out power to the entirety of Cuba after a collapse of its power grid, which left 11 million without power.

As of September 28, two people have died as a direct result of Hurricane Ian with many missing.

# United States

## Florida

Several tornado touchdowns were reported in South Florida as the storm approached on September 27, 2022, one of which severely damaged over 15 aircraft and several hangars at the North Perry Airport in Broward County.

Another tornado on the night of September 27 overturned multiple cars, shattered windows, and toppled a large tree onto an apartment building at Kings Point in Palm Beach County.

Tropical-storm-force winds were observed at Key West International Airport before 22:00 UTC (18:00 EDT) the same day; the City of Key West subsequently recorded its third-highest storm surge since 1913.

With the storm making landfall in Southwest Florida on September 27 as a strong Category 4 hurricane, the National Weather Service in Tampa issued multiple, rare extreme wind warnings, indicating the expectancy for sustained winds of 115 mph (185 km/h) or greater.

Additionally, the National Hurricane Center's advisory at 15:00 UTC warned that the "extremely dangerous eyewall of Ian" is "moving onshore." Ian's offshore flow pulled all the water out of Tampa Bay as well.

Sustained hurricane-force winds were confirmed in several places at the landfall point in Southwest Florida, including one report southeast of Cape Coral, where the location recorded a wind gust of 140 mph, around the time of Ian's second landfall.

A private weather station near Port Charlotte reported a sustained wind of 115 mph (185 km/h) with a wind gust of 132 mph (212 km/h) around the same time.

At 7:47 p.m. EDT, the National Weather Service issued a flash flood emergency for rainfall of up to 19 inches (480 mm).

Storm surge also became a serious concern for Southwest Florida, with areas between Longboat Key and Chokoloskee projected to have between 6–18 feet (1.8–5.5 m) of storm surge.

In Naples, rising coastal floodwaters trapped people and prompted numerous calls for rescue. Water entered the first floor of several parking garages, impacting many cars. A fire station was completely flooded, substantially damaging nearly all the equipment in the building. The ambulance bay and helipad were inundated at a hospital in North Naples.

Multiple rescues occurred in Goodland after some people unsuccessfully attempted to flee the storm surge. Farther inland, 4 to 6 ft (1.2 to 1.8 m) of water covered portions of U.S. Route 41 near Carnestown. The city of Venice turned off water supply to the island of Venice.

Overall, at least two million people in Florida lost electricity during the storm.

As Ian approached the state, a boat carrying 23 migrants sank. Three of them were rescued by the Coast Guard while a fourth was able to swim ashore. The remaining occupants are still missing, and it is unknown where they are currently.

# CHAPTER 34

# Lolo

Hurricane Maria was a deadly Category 5 hurricane that devastated the northeastern Caribbean in September 2017, particularly Dominica, Saint Croix, and Puerto Rico. It is regarded as the worst natural disaster in recorded history to affect those islands.

The most intense tropical cyclone worldwide in 2017, Maria was the thirteenth named storm, eighth consecutive hurricane, fourth major hurricane, second Category 5 hurricane, and deadliest storm of the extremely active 2017 Atlantic hurricane season.

Maria was the deadliest Atlantic hurricane since Mitch in 1998, and the tenth most intense Atlantic hurricane on record. Total monetary losses are estimated at upwards of $91.61 billion, 2017 U.S.D, mostly in Puerto Rico, ranking it as the third-costliest tropical cyclone on record.

Maria became a tropical storm on September 16 east of the Lesser Antilles and rapidly intensified to Category 5 strength just before making landfall in Dominica on September 18.

After crossing the island, Maria achieved its peak intensity with maximum sustained winds of 175 mph, 280 km/h, and a pressure of 908 mbar 26.81 inHg.

On September 20, an eyewall replacement cycle weakened Maria to a high-end Category 4 hurricane by the time it struck Puerto Rico.

Passing north of the Bahamas, Maria gradually degraded and weakened, swinging eastward over the open Atlantic and dissipating by October 2.

Maria brought catastrophic devastation to the entirety of Dominica, destroying housing stock and infrastructure beyond repair, and practically eradicating the island's lush vegetation. The neighboring islands of Guadeloupe and Martinique endured widespread flooding, damaged roofs, and uprooted trees.

Puerto Rico suffered catastrophic damage and a major humanitarian crisis. Most of the island's population suffered from flooding and a lack of resources, compounded by a slow relief process.

The storm caused the worst electrical blackout in U.S. history, which persisted for several months.

Maria also landed in the northeast Caribbean during relief efforts from another Category 5 hurricane, Irma, which crossed the region two weeks prior.

The total death toll is 3,059: an estimated 2,975 in Puerto Rico, 65 in Dominica, 5 in the Dominican Republic, 4 in Guadeloupe, 4 in the contiguous United States, 3 in the United States Virgin Islands, and 3 in Haiti.

Maria was the deadliest hurricane in Dominica since the 1834 Padre Ruiz hurricane and the deadliest in Puerto Rico since the 1899 San Ciriaco hurricane. This makes it the deadliest named Atlantic hurricane of the 21st century to date.

Having said that about Maria, now I will tell you some situation I went through during and after the hurricane....

Let me begin with my dad. He was 90 years old and very sick. He was screaming all the time because he wanted iced water. I told him that there was no electrical power throughout the island.

My next-door neighbor heard him and bought him a bottle of iced cold water.

*I decided to take my dad to the supermarket. In front, there were lots of people gather to talk about the hurricane. My father knew most of them.*

*There was a young lady selling coffee and other beverages. I told her to please give coffee and toast to whomever came around. I also informed her that I will pay. My dad helped the young girl, and he was happy because he was being productive. We reported every morning to our meeting place. People were there waiting for us.*

*In the meantime, I began talking to each one. They told me so many sad stories and the situation they were in.*

*I remember Matilde Rodriguez. She lives in the town of Tibes where the hurricane hit the hardest. She asked me if she needed an appointment to talk to me. I told her to please take a sit. I had a table and two chairs. People were coming from all over Ponce to talk with me.*

*My father gave them coffee. They began to relax.*

*Well, Matilde began her story, and I was devasted because she kept talking about Lolo. I let her talk and when she finished, I questioned her. Who was Lolo?*

*To my surprise, Lolo was her horse. She left Lolo locked up in a stable, however, the hurricane came also with a tornado. Lolo was thrown up in the air. He was found up on a tree.*

*Matilde lost every. Her house was destroyed, and her little farm, gone.*

*I told her that I would help her with the necessary documents. She was very happy.*

*Matilde came to my house after everything was settle. She informed me that I helped her more than any government official or family member. She also told me she got a new horse. She named him Lolo.*

*You know I did it because I saw how my beautiful island was destroyed by Hurricane Maria......*

# CHAPTER 35

# Hurricane Ian's Florida destruction

Hurricane Ian rolled over Florida last week as a powerful Category 4 storm, causing severe flooding in coastal regions due to a storm surge and torrential rains. The hurricane, which battered the coast with devastating winds of over 155 mph (250 kph), has killed nearly 100 Floridians, according to Florida Today, opens in new tab, on Monday Oct. 3, 2022.

The 2022 Atlantic hurricane season had a slow start, with no named storms forming above the ocean in the whole month of August. Since then, the activity has picked up. Just one week before Ian, Hurricane Fiona battered Porto Rico, its remnants making it all the way to Canada an unusual phenomenon that might have something to do with the climate change, according to experts.

After Hurricane Ian pummeled Florida, it regained strength over the Atlantic Ocean before making landfall for the second time in South Carolina, cutting power to 200,000 homes and causing devastating floods.

While the residues of Ian are now dropping rain over New York and New England, weather forecasters are also monitoring Tropical Storm Orlena, which made landfall as a Category 1 hurricane in southwest Mexico on Monday Oct. 3 pouring over 10 inches, 25 centimeters of rain on the coast.

A monster-sized Hurricane Ian pummeled the state on Wednesday with crushing storm surge, obliterating wind speeds and torrential rainfall, leaving a swath of devastation from the southwestern coast across the I-4 corridor.

The hurricane, the fifth-most powerful to ever hit the U.S., left countless homes and businesses wrecked or underwater and nearly 2.7 million people without power.

"Fort Myers is devastated," tweeted Dylan Federico, a meteorologist for WINK News. "Tough hurricane proof infrastructure that's in shambles. There's no electricity or water. It's unlivable. Wind damage is far worse than I saw after Irma, Ida, Harvey, or Katrina."

The death toll in Florida continued to climb. The New York Times reported Friday that officials identified at least three dozen fatalities possibly linked to the storm.

Lee County Sheriff Carmine Marceno, who initially estimated deaths in the hundreds, said there were at least 35 confirmed fatalities in the county. Six people were reported dead in Charlotte County, an elected official there also told CNN. In Volusia County, a 72-year-old man died after venturing outside to drain his pool.

Gov. Ron DeSantis said Thursday morning there were only two unconfirmed storm-related deaths, though he said more "clarity" would come over time.

"The damage done is historic," DeSantis said. "We have never seen a flood like this. We have never seen storm surge of this magnitude."

Fort Myers: 'Barely anything left'

In Lee County, the damage was so extensive and conditions on the ground so treacherous that local officials made the agonizing decision to wait before attempting certain rescues.

Lee County officials said there were a "number of calls" from people stranded by high water as flooding moved from the coast to points inland.

"It left families suffering the agony of knowing that loved one's cling to life in areas that cannot yet be reached by rescue crews because it is too dangerous to save them," said Lee County Manager Roger Desjarlais.

Fort Myers: 'Barely anything left'

In Lee County, the damage was so extensive and conditions on the ground so treacherous that local officials made the agonizing decision to wait before attempting certain rescues.

Lee County officials said there were a "number of calls" from people stranded by high water as flooding moved from the coast to points inland.

"It left families suffering the agony of knowing that loved ones cling to life in areas that cannot yet be reached by rescue crews because it is too dangerous to save them," said Lee County Manager Roger Desjarlais.

Emergency officials in Fort Myers Beach told the Tampa Bay Times that not everyone abided by evacuation orders and that they expected to find bodies as the searched through the rubble.

"Absolute devastation," said Fire Marshall Jennifer Campbell. "There's barely anything left."

Fort Myers Beach, along with Lee County's other barrier islands, took the brunt of Hurricane Ian's assault on Florida's coastline. Its commercial center, marketed as one of the most iconic areas of the town, was decimated.

From the strike zone:'Fort Myers Beach is gone': Waterfront workers recount Hurricane Ian devastation

"7-Eleven's gone. The Whale's gone. All the restaurants are gone," resident Mitch Stough told The Fort Myers News-Press. "The whole entire Times Square is gone. It's leveled."

Bonita Springs: Tears after a labor of love lost

In Bonita Springs, some structures were flattened by the storm surge, including Doc's Beach House.

The walls on Doc's Beach House caved in when the storm surge went back out, said Charlie Cibula, the owner's son, who said his father has owned it since 1987.

Nearby, his father picked through the wreckage of the restaurant's first floor, standing in the doorway. There were no walls surrounding the door frame.

We'll get it back up and running," the father said.

Doc's Beach House also suffered a propane leak, and Lee County sheriff's deputies were turning residents back, urging them to stay away and stay safe. The smell of gas wafted through the air and was noticeable blocks away.

Jason Crosser, who owns 8-Bit Hall of Fame, a classic video game store on Bonita Beach Road Southwest near the curve, lost everything. He and his wife, Erica, perched outside their shop on the empty windowsills, a cutout of Hulk Hogan next to them.

Crosser said he knew yesterday afternoon that his shop had been lost when a local news channel showed a photo of the building where his shop was located. In the photo, his shop was already halfway submerged, he said.

Crosster's eyes were rimmed with red, and he could barely keep from crying. He's lived here for 16 years and pumped every dollar back into his shop that he could, he said. It was a labor of love.

"We don't know what to do first," he said. He used to be a history teacher, he added, and said he might just move on.

"I might go back to Iowa and teach."

Kate Cimini, Naples Daily News reporter

Her biggest worry, she said, was that Fort Myers doesn't have water. She said the city lost one fire truck that got damaged during the storm after a local fire station got flooded.

City firefighters and emergency rescue personnel, she said, have been busy saving people trapped in their cars or homes due to the high flood waters. She added that most city residents followed the advice of city and state officials to evacuate flood-prone areas.

"We did have a few incidences [in which] our firefighters put themselves at risk and save members of our community," she said.

The flooding was overwhelming said, Reitman, who said city hall, which sits next to a fire station, was surrounded by water.

"It felt like there was a moat around City Hall," she said. "It was unbelievable."

Venice: Watching roofs blow off and a local landmark blasted

Bob and Mary Kuziel walked downtown Venice on Tampa Avenue searching for cell or internet Thursday morning about 8 a.m.

The Venice residents had weathered the storm in their condo on the ground floor of the nine-story Costa Brava condo building.

Bob Kuziel said they watched the rain come in sideways over Roberts Bay.

"We're trying to get in touch with people to let them know we are okay," Mary Kuziel said.

Instead, they found Venice Little Theater devastated by Hurricane Ian. The near-Category 5 storm had ripped through the local landmark just over the north bridge to the island of Venice.

Bob Kuziel said his grandkids have attended drama camp at the theater and it's a great place for seniors to spend time. He said it was sad to see it in this state.

While the fear had been that storm surge would plunge Venice under feet of water, it appears Ian's worst damage has come from winds in Venice.

At the Municipal Airport Mobile Home Park, many trailers had extensive roof damage. Cotton-candy pink insulation and twisted metal roof debris was strewn throughout the property.

Doris Welch has owned a manufactured home in the park since 1997, but only owned the mobile home—where the aluminum roof was now peeled like an orange—since 2005.

She said she weathered the storm at a friend's property about 10 minutes away. But on the ride over she worried that her property would be flattened.

"We know what mother nature can do with winds that high," she said. "It was inevitable."

While the damage looked bad, with parts of the roof flipped back, Welch thought the majority of the roof held and expected that it wasn't too severe.

Venice Municipal Airport, about half-mile from the mobile home park, had severe damage to several hangers.

"I lost two planes," Andre Ghawi said. "They were in the hangar. The hangar doesn't exist anymore. You don't figure on something like this happening."

Meanwhile, Wayne LeBlanc spent Thursday morning picking up parts of his neighbor's roof at the Venice Municipal Mobile Home Park. He said he hunkered down in his trailer when Ian struck.

"Three-quarters of the way thru, I was wishing I hadn't. I watched roofs get ripped off." he said.

North Port: Eight hours of destruction with a 'horrendous' soundtrack

In this North Port community, hundreds of homes were destroyed by Hurricane Ian.

George and Sharon Fink weathered Hurricane Ian in their manufactured home in North Port, only to realize Thursday morning that their house was one of few spared by the Category 4 storm that tore through the community.

The Fink's live in Holiday Park, a retiree community in North Port with 836 manufactured homes that was devastated on Wednesday by winds that topped 100 miles per hour. Hundreds of homes were destroyed, but theirs stood tall on Thursday morning.

"The noise was horrendous," Sharon, 74, said. "The noise reminded me of being at a stock car race, and the engines are revving. That is what the wind sounded like. The roar from the stock cars, that's what it sounded like. It was nonstop, wind just blowing and blowing. It was like that for like 8 hours."

Hundreds of thousands without power in Florida as Ian death toll climbs

The death toll from Hurricane Ian has risen to 84, days after it pummeled Florida's western coast as a major storm before barreling through the Carolinas, according to AP.

The latest: More than 344,000 customers were without power in Florida on Tuesday night as affected states continued with recovery efforts in the aftermath of last week's hurricane. That's down from almost 414,000 customers the day before.

Of those confirmed dead, 75 were in Florida, another five occurred in North Carolina and one death was recorded in Virginia, per AP. Another three people died in Cuba because of the storm.

Floodwaters were starting to recede in many places. But the National Weather Service office in Melbourne said on Tuesday night flooding and standing water issues in central Florida would continue for "several more days."

The big picture: Ian made landfall as a high-end Category 4 storm in Florida last Wednesday. On Friday, it made landfall in South Carolina as a Category 1 storm, carrying a "life-threatening" storm surge of 4 to 7 feet, Axios' Andrew Freedman writes.

Officials in Florida said over 2,350 people had been rescued in the state as of Monday.

The storm had regained hurricane status on Thursday night on its way to a damaging encounter with the Carolinas and a portion of southern Georgia.

State of play: "This is going to be a long road to recovery and there are a lot of people that are impacted," Federal Emergency Management Agency (FEMA) Administrator Deanne Criswell told ABC's "This Week" on Sunday.

Florida Gov. Ron DeSantis announced Tuesday officials had opened a disaster recovery center in Fort Myers, which was pummeled by Hurricane Ian.

"This center is a one-stop-shop, bringing together 10 state and federal agencies to help Floridians get back on their feet," he tweeted. "More locations will be opening soon."

Sen. Marco Rubio (R-Fla.) told ABC's "This Week" on Sunday there had been "an extraordinary mobilization of the army corps, the coast guard, I mean virtually every federal asset that's available, not just through FEMA but other agencies," Rubio added.

Of note: President Biden, who's due to meet with DeSantis during a visit to Florida on Wednesday, noted last week that the hurricane "is likely to rank among the worst in the nation's history."

"You have all seen on television homes and property wiped out. It's going to take months, years to rebuild," he said.

For the record: NHC officials noted Thursday that many hurricane-related deaths occur days after the storm has passed while people are recovering.

These deaths, also called "indirect deaths," primarily arise from excessive heat and over-exertion and carbon monoxide poisoning from running generators indoors.

## How Hurricane Ian caught so many off guard

Hurricane Ian was a nightmare of a storm to forecast, and experts say the tools meteorologists used to assess and communicate its likely path were part of the problem.

Why it matters: With the death toll mounting, meteorologists, emergency managers and others are asking how they could have done a better job making clear the storm would devastate the Ft. Myers area and what lessons they can learn for the next storm.

# RESOURCES

1.  Atlantic Oceanographic and Meteorological Laboratory, Hurricane Research Division. "Frequently Asked Questions: When is hurricane season?". NOAA. Archived from the original on July 18, 2006. Retrieved July 25, 2006.
2.  McAdie, Colin May 10, 2007. "Tropical Cyclone Climatology". National Hurricane Center. Archived from the original on May 28, 2007. Retrieved June 9, 2007.
3.  "Atlantic hurricane best track HURDAT version 2". Hurricane Research Division (Database). Miami, FL: National Hurricane Center. April 11, 2017. Retrieved November 1, 2017.
4.  Associated Press, June 15, 1941. "Hurricane Bureau Begins Season's Vigil Tonight". St. Petersburg Times. Retrieved July 9, 2011.
5.  Associated Press, June 15, 1959. "1959 Hurricane Season Opens Officially Today". Meridian Record. Retrieved July 9, 2011.
6.  Associated Press June 15, 1955. "Hurricane Season Opens; New England Joins Circuit". The Robesonian. Retrieved July 9, 2011.
7.  Associated Press, June 15, 1960. "1960 Hurricane Season Open As Planes Prowl". The Evening Independent. Retrieved July 9, 2011.
8.  Neal Dorst, January 21, 2010. "Subject: G1 When is hurricane season?". National Hurricane Center. Archived from the original on June 28, 2011. Retrieved July 9, 2011.
9.  Brownsville Herald, June 1, 1965. Hurricane Season Officially Opened.

10. United Press International (May 30, 1966). "Hurricane Season Opens This Week". The News and Courier. Retrieved July 9, 2011.

11. National Hurricane Center, 2011. "Atlantic Graphical Tropical Weather Outlook". National Oceanic and Atmospheric Administration. Archived from the original on June 23, 2011. Retrieved July 9, 2011.

12. United States Department of Commerce, 2006. Assessment: Hurricane Katrina, August 23–31, 2005. Retrieved on 2008-09-03.

13. Hurricane Research Division (2008). "Chronological List of All Hurricanes which Affected the Continental United States: 1851-2007". National Oceanic and Atmospheric Administration. Retrieved March 21, 2008.

14. Dorst, Neal, October 23, 2012. "They Called the Wind Mahina: The History of Naming Cyclones" (PPTX). Hurricane Research Division, Atlantic Oceanographic and Meteorological Laboratory. National Oceanic and Atmospheric Administration. p. Slides 49–51.

15. Wang and Gilles 2011. "Observed Change in Sahel Rainfall, Circulations, African Easter

16. Arya, Manish. "Puerto Rico raises Hurricane Maria death toll to 34". Consumer Info line. Retrieved October 4, 2017.

17. Nicole Friedman, September 25, 2017. "Hurricane Maria Caused as Much as $85 Billion in Insured Losses, AIR Worldwide Says". The Wall Street Journal. Retrieved September 26, 2017.

18. "Wide Variations in Hurricane Maria Damage Estimates in Puerto Rico". Caribbean Business. October 6, 2017. Retrieved October 7, 2017.

19. September 28, 2017. "Hurricane Maria could be a $95 billion storm for Puerto Rico". CNN Money. Retrieved October 8, 2017.

20. Brennan, Michael, September 13, 2017. "Graphical Tropical Weather Outlook". National Hurricane Center. Retrieved September 17, 2017.

21. Blake, Eric, September 14, 2017. "Graphical Tropical Weather Outlook". National Hurricane Center. Retrieved September 17, 2017.

22. Blake, Eric, September 15, 2017. "Graphical Tropical Weather Outlook". National Hurricane Center. Retrieved September 17, 2017.

23. a b Cangialosi, John September 16, 2017. "Potential Tropical Cyclone Fifteen Discussion Number 1". National Hurricane Center. Retrieved September 20, 2017.

24. Henson, Bob (June 18, 2017). "NHC Unveils New Product with Potential Tropical Cyclone in Atlantic". Weather Underground. Retrieved rly Waves, and Atlantic Hurricanes Since

25. López, Alberto; Hughes, K. Stephen; Vanacore, Elizabeth (2020). 26. "Puerto Rico's Winter 2019-2020 Seismic Sequence Leaves the Island on Edge". Temblor. doi:10.32858/temblor.064.

26. "USGS 6.4 Puerto Rico (tectonic summary)". earthquake.usgs.gov. Retrieved 2020-07-30.

27. Trafecante, Kate (7 January 2020). "Analyst says earthquakes could cost Puerto Rico's economy up to $3.1 billion". CNN. Retrieved 11 January 2020.

28. Puerto Rico residents fear aftershocks after deadly 6.4 magnitude earthquake. David Begnaud. CBS NEWS. January 7, 2020. Accessed 31 January 2020.

29. You tube, and History channel has a lot of information on Nature Rage

30. Magnitude 5.9 earthquake rocks Puerto Rico and causes landslide in Peñuelas. Grace Hauck. USA TODAY. 11 January 2020. Accessed 14 January 2020.

31. ANSS (January 31, 2019). "Search results". Retrieved January 31, 2019.

32. ANSS. "Puerto Rico 2020: M 6.4–8km S of Indios, Puerto Rico". Comprehensive Catalog. U.S. Geological Survey. Retrieved January 7, 2020.

33. "INFORME DE LA ACTIVIDAD SÍSMICA EN LA REGIÓN DE PUERTO RICO E ISLAS VÍRGENES DURANTE EL MES DE MARZO DE 2022" (PDF) (in Spanish). Retrieved 2022-08-27. Este temblor fuerte, con profundidad de 7 km, tuvo una intensidad máxima de VIII en Guánica, Puerto Rico y produjo daños mayores a través de Puerto Rico. This strong tremor, with a depth of 7 km, had a maximum intensity of VIII in Guánica, Puerto Rico and produced major damage throughout Puerto Rico.

34. "Confirman la primera muerte por el temblor en Ponce". El Nuevo Dia (in Spanish). 2020-01-07. Retrieved 2020-01-07. d 13 January 2020.

# ABOUT THE AUTHOR

Norma Iris Pagan Morales was born in Ponce, Puerto Rico. Her parents, Juan Jose Pagan Rodriguez, and Digna Morales Figueroa, now deceased, always helped her with her projects as a writer and teaching career.

Norma had three siblings, Adelin Milagros Pagan Morales, Juan Jose Pagan Morales, and Julio Manuel Pagan Morales. Julio Manuel Pagan Morales died on September 19, 1998. He was also known for his writing / composer skills.

Norma did all her academic studies in New York City, Puerto Rico, and Canada. She worked in the City of New York Police Department where she oversaw the full investigation of every new civilian and uniform member of the department.

As an Educator, she worked in New York City Bd. of Education, in Puerto Rico Bd. of Education as an English teacher. She also worked for the Puerto Rico Army National as an English Teacher.

She has teaching certifications for English as a Second Language and Teaching English as a Foreign Language. She also has teaching licenses to teach the following:

1. English Literature
2. Spanish Literature
3. Communication Skills in both English and Spanish
4. Office Procedures= These classes consisted of basic filing to writing memorandums and full company or organization reports.
5. Computers - Certified to teach Long Distance Learning

She has published Seven books: Proud of My Puerto Rican Bequest, Porque Soy Boricua? Poemas del Alma, Art in Written Form, A Baffling Short Stories Collection and On Job in the Big Apple

www.ingramcontent.com/pod-product-compliance
Lightning Source LLC
Chambersburg PA
CBHW032053020426
42335CB00011B/321